"In my opinion, this cookbook is long overdue. I don't know that I've met a person who cares more deeply for sharing the simple joys of food with others as Andrea does. Her recipes are thoughtful and delicious without complication or bizarre ingredients. These recipes are staples, not once-attempted extravagances, and they will no doubt earn a place in your home as they have in mine."
JULIE BUSHA, President, Slawsa, *Progressive Grocer* 2015 "Top Women in Grocery"

"Looking for a modern twist on Southern Cooking? Look no further than *Cooktales: A Keepsake Cookbook* by Andrea LeTard where she shares not only the delicious recipes but the stories, people and emotions behind each dish. Andrea highlights many recipes handed down to her from her grandmother that are true heirlooms in her family and gives you an area to save your family's special dishes. This cookbook is a great way to spice up your family meals and a treasure for anyone who wants to start gathering their own keepsake recipes. Crack open *Cooktales: A Keepsake Cookbook*, pour yourself a glass of wine and get cooking!"
LAURIE FORSTER, TheWineCoach.com and author of *The Sipping Point: A Crash Course in Wine*

"When I read through Andrea's recipes and tales, I imagine her and her friends and family gathered together in her kitchen and at her table … with laughter and love in full swing. And of course, creating memories and stories that won't soon be forgotten. Each tale reminds me of recipes and meals I have enjoyed with those I love. As Andrea encourages, I look forward to taking notes and journaling when preparing her recipes. I know her dishes are going to help me — and everyone who cooks from this book - create some pretty delicious memories."
JENNIFER CHANDLER, author of *The Southern Pantry Cookbook, Simply Grilling, Simply Suppers*, and *Simply Salads*

"Andrea's talents are uniquely showcased in this cookbook that will surely enlighten and entertain all culinary fans across the board. Her expertise is exposed through her creativity and preparations and culminate with recipes that are delicious and fun to concoct! Culinary experts to the novice cook will be enlightend and entertained!"
WALKER TAYLOR, Commissary BBQ Restaurants

"Andrea is an expert at making healthy food taste delicious, and we are lucky to have her consult with us on our menus. She has opened our eyes to a whole new world of flavor. Her recipes reflect her passion for the process and her enthusiasm for nourishment from the inside out."
BROWN DUDLEY, Owner, Soli

Lucy —

Have fun,
Eat Happy!

Andrea's
COOKTALES

A Keepsake Cookbook
Learn New Recipes, Treasure Old Ones

Andrea Letard

by ANDREA LETARD

PHOTOGRAPHY by NICOLE COLE
FOREWORD by JENNIFER CHANDLER
EDITED by SUSAN SCHADT

SUSAN SCHADT PRESS

Memphis | New Orleans

To Tres,
My Once Upon a Time,
Happily Ever After,
and everything in between.

"You and I have been happy; we haven't been happy just once, we've been happy a thousand times." - F. SCOTT FITZGERALD

The Plot
ANDREA'S COOKTALES

🕐 *Make ahead dishes and tips*

📌 *Helpful hints and tips*

📷 Tag me on Instagram with your Andrea's Cooktales creations and any food pictures and stories you'd like to share - **@andreas_cooktales** #andreascooktales

by JENNIFER CHANDLER

FOREWORD

So much of Southern living is spent in the kitchen and around the dinner table. My most cherished memories are centered on a meal.

My dad's family is from New Orleans and, in my honest opinion, his mom was the best cook in the world. This demure French Creole woman could cook up a storm. I don't think I ever had a meal from her kitchen that was not delicious. I have vivid memories of standing on my tip-toes to peer into the pots simmering on her stove-top, helping her slice the French bread, and giggling with my cousins at the kids' table.

Today my favorite meals are the ones where my guests at my table - whether family or friends - are in the kitchen with me helping bring it all together. We all throw on aprons and start cooking. My friends, family, and even the kids help with the prep and to set the table. Standing around the kitchen island, we laugh, tell stories and catch-up. Sometimes the meal is fancy; most often not. But is always good food made with love.

When I read through Andrea's recipes and tales, I imagine her and her friends and family gathered together in her kitchen and at her table ... with laughter and love in full swing. And of course, creating memories and stories that won't soon be forgotten. Each tale reminds me of recipes and meals I have enjoyed with those I love.

The recipes that Andrea shares with you in this book are those of family traditions. Recipes passed down from her own parents and grandparents as well as new dishes that have become traditions for her and her husband, recipes that remind us of how a meal can bring the comfort of good food and good company. No fancy restaurant in the world can offer up food as good as what is made in a Southern kitchen with love.

Andrea's recipes are simple to prepare but filled with fun and interesting twists that will excite both the beginner and the experienced cook. Dishes like Buffalo Hot Wing Hummus and Balsamic BBQ Meatballs will help you get the party started. Brown Sugar Short Ribs and Caribbean Seared Tuna with Mojito Sauce will become your entertaining go-tos. And for the perfect endings, you will be asking for seconds of desserts like Nenne's Famous Pecan Pie, a dish she learned from her grandmother, and Vanilla Berry Shortcake.

As Andrea encourages, I look forward to taking notes and journaling when preparing her recipes. I know her dishes are going to help me – and everyone who cooks from this book - create some pretty delicious memories.

Jennifer Chandler is the author of *The Southern Pantry Cookbook, Simply Grilling, Simply Suppers,* and *Simply Salads.*

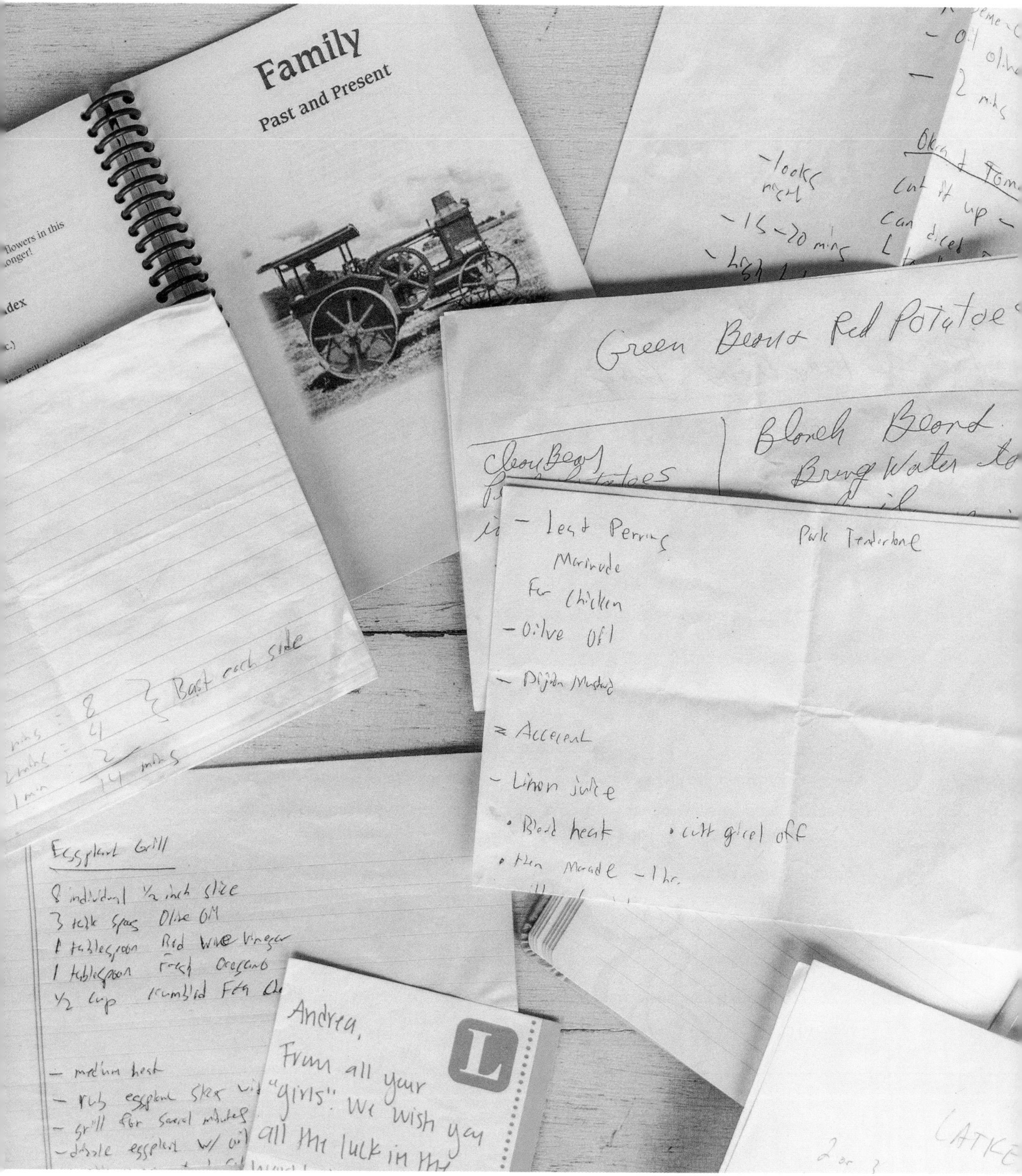

Family

Past and Present

flowers in this

onger!

dex

c)

—looks
rich
—15-20 mins

Okra & Tom
Cut it up
can diced

Green Bean & Red Potatoes

Clean Beans
Potatoes

Blanch Beans
Bring Water to

— Lea & Perrins
Marinade
For Chicken

Pork Tenderloin

— Olive Oil

— Dijon Mustard

= Acccent

— Lemon Juice

• Blend heat   • cut glreel off

• thin Marinade — 1 hr

mins =   8
         4   } Baste each side
whole = 2
1 min   14 mins

Eggplant Grill

8 individual ½ inch slice
3 table spoons Olive Oil
1 tablespoon Red Wine Vinegar
1 tablespoon Fresh Oregano
½ cup   crumbled Feta Ch

— medium heat
— rub eggplant slice wi
— grill for several minutes
— drizzle eggplant w/ oil

Andrea,
From all your
"girls". We wish you
all the luck in the

L

LATKE

2 or 3

by ANDREA LETARD

INTRODUCTION

When you look at a recipe, what do you see? Maybe you see the ingredients, the directions, yourself in the kitchen, a beautifully plated dish or your family and friends devouring the finished product? Like most cooks, when I choose a recipe I too envision the process from beginning to end. But I see more. In every recipe I run across, I see life – stories, memories, experiences. I see history – where the recipes were discovered, the people behind them, the families who shared them. I see love – a table of family or friends laughing over wine, the memories made with every pot stirred and bite taken and generations of cooking passed down over many years. A recipe is more than just a dish – there's a story behind each one. Food is the centerpiece of all things worth celebrating.

This cookbook is full of stories and memories from my own kitchen and dinner table, but I also want it to be a journal and a home for your own kitchen stories, cooking memories and family recipes. We all have hand-written recipes from our mothers, grandmothers or great-grandmothers; favorite recipes saved on our computer or phone; cooking tips passed down from family members or friends; and celebrations over food we simply wish to never forget. My wish is that you will keep them here, and along the way, I hope some of my own stories and recipes encourage you to continue cooking and making memories around the dinner table. Food is in our hearts and souls – yes, because we need it to survive, and it tastes good, but it's only as good as the people we share it with and the memories that are created through it. May this cookbook be an inspiration, a keepsake and an heirloom for years to come.

My recipes are what I call "next generation southern" - fun and fundamentally southern with a modern twist, using fine, fresh, and sometimes unexpected ingredients. In this book, you'll find eighty recipes in various forms. Some are clean and healthy, while others are full of naughty deliciousness. Some are quick weekday meals, while others are perfect for a loungy weekend at home. Some are easy as pie, while others are a bit challenging (but I promise, not hard) when you want to test your skills in the kitchen. And those other recipes - the ones you add - are whatever you want them to be. I hope they're your most prized possessions, and they make you happy every time you look at them.

What is Cooktales?

Several years ago, before I ever stepped foot in any kitchen, my dad's side of the family had a cookbook made. Each member of the family contributed passed down recipes, and my grandmother, Mammaw, included several of her most famous recipes that I loved as a child. I discovered some of these recipes dated all the way back to the 1800s. Mammaw gave me a copy of the cookbook, and when I realized that in my very hands, I had the best ravioli recipe in the entire world, I decided it was time to learn to cook.

That cookbook was the beginning of a passion and talent I never knew I had, and it became somewhat of a guide for my cooking future. As I flipped through the pages, looking at old family pictures, discovering unique ingredients and reading through a chapter called "Depression Years," it hit me: there's a story behind every recipe. For every recipe that exists today, there are numerous stories and small pieces of history that played into its creation. As I started writing my own recipes, I kept seeing that same pattern. Every recipe I created was influenced by a childhood memory, a vacation taken, a night with my husband, fun with my friends – I never wrote a recipe just to write one, there was always an experience that made me want to write it. It was then, I started calling my recipes *Cooktales* and decided to start my blog, *Andrea's Cooktales*.

Though not an actual word that can be looked up in the dictionary and defined, the word Cooktales has a strong meaning. It's about storytelling from the kitchen and the dinner table. It's memories around food that are meaningful and worth savoring. Cooktales is sitting at the kitchen table snapping green beans with your grandma, watching your mom make her special spaghetti sauce and hoping one day you'll be able to make it exactly the same. It is memories of waking up on Saturday morning to your dad's famous pancakes, happy hour with friends on a Thursday night because you can't wait for the

weekend, Sunday cookouts in the summer, sitting on a patio with the person you love - glasses of wine and a cheese plate between you - laughing and soaking up the sun. And mostly, it's what you look forward to every day after several long hours of work, when you get to come home to your family, sit down at the dinner table, talk about your day and unwind. Cooktales is about more than just food, it's about life.

My Cooktales

Remember in the TV show *Sex and the City* when Carrie jokes about her oven being storage space? That was me in my twenties. I went from someone in her early twenties who never stepped foot in the kitchen to someone now, in my thirties, who has made a career out of cooking. After several years of cooking and falling in love with it, I had an epiphany and wondered if I could ever make a living out of this fun hobby I'd picked up. It didn't seem possible - after all, don't all chefs go to culinary school? Don't they all claim they've been cooking since childhood? Don't they all have restaurant experience? I didn't have any of these credentials, and at the time, it was extremely discouraging. But then it dawned on me - lots of successful "chefs" were actually home cooks who didn't start their careers in the kitchen until later in life. Julia Child didn't discover her love for food or start cooking until she was in her forties. Ina Garten, without a culinary degree, quit her full-time job and opened a specialty food store when she was in her thirties.

Sure, I wasn't a chef. But like these ladies, I was a home cook who happened upon a cooking career because I took a chance on something I absolutely love. The truth is, there's a lot you can teach yourself about something if you have a strong enough passion for it.

When I first started my cooking business, I was asked a lot where I went to culinary school. I hated that question and remember the feeling of dread when I had to explain myself as a "self-taught chef," but it wasn't long until I realized people didn't look down on me for it. They respected it and were impressed by my perseverance. Despite the late start in life, I had turned a passion into a career - something anyone can do with a lot of determination and hard work.

My story begins as a writer - not a chef. I always loved to write, and I said at a very young age that one day I wanted to have a book published. Little did I know, that book would be a cookbook. With a bachelor's degree in speech, communication and journalism, I took a job out of college as the writer and editor for a website. Six years later, I left that job and started graduate school, focusing my time on writing and studying, but I discovered I had more time on my hands than I ever imagined. This was at the same time my grandmother gave me the family cookbook, so sure enough, I spent that extra time in the kitchen. When I wasn't cooking, I was watching cooking shows, reading cookbooks and searching the Internet for all-things food - cooking went from an occasional way to kill time to an all-out obsession.

Not long after I found my new hobby, another job fell in my lap that had nothing to do with writing or cooking, but the money was fabulous, so I took it. I became a pharmaceutical sales rep. I was working full-time, going to graduate school part-time and cooking *all the time*. I started writing my own recipes and would occasionally post them on Facebook. I had so many requests from friends to start a recipe blog, so I decided that would be my ultimate goal when I finished graduate school. I literally couldn't wait - the day I had my master's degree in hand, I posted my first recipe online. I continued working in pharmaceutical sales, but my cooking passion never slowed and every spare second I had,

I was researching, testing and writing about food. During the week, I would often pay a visit to Porcellino's, one of my favorite Memphis restaurants, for lunch or coffee. I would sit in the charming little place in my pencil skirt and heels, sipping a cappuccino and watch through the bakery and butcher windows, hoping that one day I could trade my blazer for an apron. It wasn't long until I did just that.

My validation came when I combined my two loves - cooking and television. As a journalism major, my internship was in broadcasting, and on-camera work was something I always enjoyed. My blog became the home for a video series, and I became a regular contributor on a local morning show in Memphis doing cooking demos. Then the unthinkable happened. *MasterChef* auditions came to Memphis, and friends and family urged me to "just show up and see what happens." I loved cooking on camera, but never in a million years did I think I would audition for a reality show. It seemed so silly, but I've always been told to never pass up an opportunity that could be the path to the future, so I did it.

The Saturday of tryouts, I had a friend in town for a beer festival, so auditioning for a reality television show was the last thing I wanted to do. Nevertheless, I found myself standing in a hotel ballroom full of *MasterChef* hopefuls with my Le Creuset dutch oven full of Brown Sugar Braised Short Ribs (page 158) and my saucepan of Cream Cheese Grits (page 26) sitting in front of me - ready to be plated together and judged. Then a funny thing happened. I was advanced to the next round, then the next and then the final round (so much for the beer fest - seriously, I missed the whole thing). Weeks later, I had been through in-person interviews, on-camera interviews, a home video and lots of back and forth emails - just to name the half of it. Next thing I knew, I was invited to Los Angeles and given the title, along with ninety-nine others, "Top 100 Home Cooks in America." *MasterChef* flew all one hundred of us to Los Angeles for a final audition before choosing the top forty that would be competing on the show. While I didn't make it on the show, I left the audition validated, knowing I had a future career in cooking.

Being chosen as a Top Home Cook in America out of 40,000 people who auditioned was a complete stamp of approval for me. When I got home, Tres and I discussed the evolution of *Andrea's Cooktales* and the potential business opportunity. We toyed with the idea for several months, and one day Tres said to me, "If you want to do this full-time, you have my support." I never looked back. I stopped working in a career where the money made me happy and started working in one where what I was doing made me happy.

Once Upon a Time
BREAKFAST & BRUNCH

"La-di-da, little Miss Astor."

Because I grew up in the Deep South – and perhaps the 80s and 90s – we ate breakfast from early morning until lunch began at noon. What I'm trying to say is, brunch was not "a thing" in my younger days. While I knew it existed, I thought it was something only fancy people ate. As a matter of fact, I can hear my Nenne's voice now, mocking the brunchers of the world, "Ohhhh bruuuunch, well La-di-da, little Miss Astor." Little Miss Astor was Nenne's favorite nickname for me as a child when I was prancing around acting prissy – the last thing anyone wanted us to be in our silly, fun, light-hearted family was bratty or pretentious.

Fast-forward to my college years, and brunch was still nonexistent. I went to school at Delta State University in the Mississippi Delta, and when my sorority sisters and I rolled out of bed on the weekends between the hours of eleven and one, our options were down-home, country-style buffets or one of the little sandwich cafes on the square. Not a mimosa or eggs benedict to be had. Laugh all you want, but we didn't only like it – we loved it. I still miss waking up, eating bottomless fried chicken, okra and macaroni and cheese, and then rolling back into our sorority hall dorm beds – usually piled on top of each other – to watch episodes of our *Sex and the City* DVD box sets (*Netflix* and *Hulu* didn't exist) until the sun went down and it was time to go out again. Those were the days, and it wasn't the life Miss Astor lived, I assure you. But it was the best, most cherished life that none of my girls nor I will ever forget.

I don't know when brunch became such an ordinary meal for the common folk, but today it seems like no matter what you're eating on a Saturday or Sunday from the hours of ten to three, no one is calling it breakfast or lunch – it's brunch. Whatever you choose to call it, this chapter salutes those slow, easy weekend brunch mornings with a couple of quick, easy breakfast ideas for the busy week.

Fried Chicken and Corncakes

Do you have a "death row" meal? You know, the meal you would choose to be your last if you were on death row. This is an inside joke my girlfriends and I have had since college. Every time one of us eats something amazing, it's loudly and proudly proclaimed, "Oh my gosh, y'all! This is my death row meal!" Our death row meals are always changing, but I have decided my official one is Chicken and Waffles – with a side of cheese grits. The first time I wanted to make Chicken and Waffles at home, I didn't have a waffle maker so I had to get creative. Being that cornbread is a southern staple that goes great with fried chicken, I decided to replace waffles with corncakes. This dish is a perfect combination of sweet, spicy, and savory. Plus, frying the rosemary takes it to a whole other level.

Make the chicken. Place the chicken in a large bowl and cover with 1 cup of buttermilk.

🕐 *Cover with plastic wrap and refrigerate for several hours or overnight.* When ready to fry, heat 2 inches of vegetable oil in a large cast iron pan to 375 degrees. In a large, shallow bowl, pour in the remaining cup of buttermilk. In a large paper or plastic grocery bag, shake together the flour, garlic powder, minced rosemary, salt, cayenne, and pepper. Drain the buttermilk from the chicken. Working with about 4 to 5 chicken tenderloins at a time, place the pieces into the bag with the flour mixture, close, and shake until coated. Dip each floured piece into the clean bowl of buttermilk, then shake one more time in the flour mixture. Fry in batches of 4 to 5 strips for about 6 to 8 minutes, or until cooked through and golden. Drain on a paper towel-lined baking sheet. Once all the chicken is fried, fry the rosemary sprigs for 1 to 2 minutes. Set aside with the chicken.

Make the corncakes. In a large bowl, whisk together the flour, cornmeal, sugar, baking powder, baking soda, and salt until combined. In a medium bowl, beat together the eggs, buttermilk, honey, butter, and sour cream until smooth. Pour the wet ingredients into the dry ingredients and whisk together to form a smooth batter. *This can be done ahead of time and refrigerated for up to 2 days.* On a buttered skillet set over medium heat, fry your corncakes in batches – the same way you do pancakes - until golden and cooked through on each side – using about 1/3 cup of batter for each corncake.

Make the syrup. Whisk together the pepper jelly and maple syrup in a small bowl and microwave for several minutes. *This can also be done several days before and reheated before serving.* Serve "family-style" by arranging the corncakes on a large platter with the chicken and rosemary on top. Pour some of the hot pepper syrup all over the chicken and corncakes. Serve the remaining syrup on the side.

Notes

Serves 4 to 6

CHICKEN:

- 2 pounds chicken tenderloins
- 2 cups buttermilk
- Vegetable oil - for frying
- 2 ½ cups all-purpose flour
- 2 tablespoons garlic powder
- 1 tablespoon minced fresh rosemary
- 1 tablespoon kosher salt
- ½ tablespoon cayenne
- ½ teaspoon freshly ground black pepper
- 6 to 8 large sprigs fresh rosemary

CORNCAKES:

- 1 ½ cups all-purpose flour
- ¾ cup cornmeal
- ⅓ cup granulated sugar
- 1 teaspoon baking powder
- ½ teaspoon baking soda
- ½ teaspoon kosher salt
- 2 large eggs
- 1 ¼ cups buttermilk
- 1 tablespoon honey
- ½ stick unsalted butter – melted, plus more for the skillet
- ½ cup sour cream

SYRUP:

- 2 tablespoons hot pepper jelly
- 1 cup good-quality maple syrup

Brussels and Date Frittata with Crispy Prosciutto

Frittatas are a weekly staple for my husband, Tres and me. We eat them for breakfast, brunch, and dinner. They're quick, easy, typically healthy, plus we always have eggs and veggies on hand. One night, I didn't particularly feel like going to the grocery store. All we had were eggs, brussels sprouts and prosciutto so I decided that would be our dinner. As I was throwing it together, dates caught my eye, and as odd as it seemed, something told me to put them in the dish. The flavor combo sounds insane, but it surprisingly works and the dates are a fun little surprise in each bite. This is now our favorite frittata and I learned that sometimes a trip to the grocery store is completely unnecessary.

Preheat your oven to 400 degrees. In an oven-proof sauté pan, heat the olive oil and butter over medium heat. Add the shallots and cook for about 2 minutes, or until they start to brown. Stir in the Brussels sprouts and season with ½ teaspoon salt and ½ teaspoon pepper. Using a spatula, press down and let cook for several minutes until crispy and brown. Flip the Brussels and cook on the other side, pressing down, until crisp and golden.

Turn the heat down to low. In a large bowl, whisk together the eggs, half-and-half, 1 teaspoon salt, and ½ teaspoon pepper. Fold in the Parmesan, goat cheese, and dates. Pour the egg mixture over the Brussels and stir until some of the egg is cooked. As the egg cooks on the outside of the pan, push the cooked egg to the center. Do this over the stove for about 2 minutes, making sure the Brussels and dates are evenly distributed. Layer the prosciutto over the egg mixture and place in the oven for 10 to 12 minutes, or until egg mixture is cooked through and the prosciutto is crispy.

Serves 4 to 6

- 1 tablespoon olive oil
- 1 tablespoon unsalted butter
- 2 shallots – sliced
- ½ pound Brussels sprouts – sliced thin
- Kosher salt and freshly ground black pepper
- 8 large eggs
- ¼ cup half-and-half
- ¼ cup freshly grated Parmesan
- 2 ounces goat cheese
- 6 dates – pitted and chopped
- 3 to 4 ounces prosciutto slices

Notes

....

....

....

....

....

....

"Don't Be Ugly" Grits 'N Greens Bowl

Cheese grits should only be served extra creamy. Period. And I'm not going to sugar coat it, if I'm served dry grits in a restaurant – which happens more than you'd think – I send them right back. I avoid sending food back at all costs, but if something isn't right, I see no problem with it. My girlfriends have always been mortified when I do this and as considerate as I am about it, they always feel the need to remind me to be nice. I recall the exact words, "Don't be ugly now," coming from a couple of them on more than one occasion. So when I make grits at home – extra creamy – I always think about this and it makes me laugh. These grits are so velvety and flavorful, there's nothing to "be ugly" about when you eat them. The greens and bacon gravy turn this succulent side dish into a meal and the flavor combo is unreal. Top with roasted shrimp, blackened fish, or fried chicken, and you'll slap mama.

Make the greens. In a large sauté pan, heat the butter over medium-low heat. Add the minced garlic and red pepper flakes and cook for one minute, or until fragrant. Add the sliced greens, salt, and pepper. Stir together and let wilt down for about two minutes. Pour in the cider vinegar and sugar and stir together. Simmer until the vinegar is reduced by half. Raise the heat to high, add the chicken stock and apple juice, let come to a slight boil, and then lower the heat. Cover and let simmer for about 30 minutes, or until time to plate.

Recipe continues on next page.

Serves 4

GREENS:

- 2 tablespoons unsalted butter
- 2 garlic cloves – minced
- ¼ teaspoon red pepper flakes
- 2 large bunches of fresh greens (collards, turnips, or mustard) – rinsed, dried, stems removed, and thinly sliced
- ½ teaspoon kosher salt
- ¼ teaspoon freshly ground black pepper
- ½ cup apple cider vinegar
- ½ teaspoon granulated sugar
- 2 cups low-sodium chicken stock
- 2 cups apple juice

Notes

25

"Don't Be Ugly" Grits 'N Greens Bowl (*cont.*)

While the greens are cooking, start the grits. In a large saucepan, heat the chicken stock and milk over medium heat. When warm, start whisking in the grits slowly. Then season with the salt and pepper. When the grits start to boil slightly, lower the heat. Cover and let simmer for about 15 to 20 minutes, uncovering and whisking occasionally. If they get too dry, thin them out with more milk. Stir in the cream cheese and butter until melted. Taste and add more salt if needed. The end-product should be an extra-creamy consistency.

🕐 *They can be made up to 2 days ahead and refrigerated. Reheat on the stovetop, adding more stock or milk as you whisk to keep them smooth and creamy.*

While the grits are cooking, make the gravy. In a medium sauté pan, fry the bacon until crispy. Drain on a paper towel-lined plate, retaining the bacon grease. Over medium heat, whisk the flour into the bacon grease until the mixture is smooth and light brown in color, watching carefully so it doesn't burn. Slowly whisk in about half of the chicken stock. When it starts to bubble and thicken, simmer and stir in the paprika, red pepper flakes, and salt. Let simmer for 5 to 10 minutes until thick. If it gets too thick, whisk in more stock. Before serving, stir in the butter until melted.

To plate, spoon grits in the bottom of 4 shallow bowls, top with the greens, spoon the gravy over the top, and finish with a sprinkle of the chopped bacon. You can also serve family-style in a large bowl.

GRITS:

- 2 cups low-sodium chicken stock
- 2 cups whole milk, plus more for thinning
- 1 cup stone-ground grits
- 1 ½ teaspoons kosher salt, plus more to taste
- 1 teaspoon freshly ground black pepper
- 6 ounces cream cheese
- 2 tablespoons unsalted butter

GRAVY:

- 6 slices of thick-cut bacon – sliced
- 3 tablespoons all-purpose flour
- 1 to 2 cups low-sodium chicken stock
- 1 teaspoon smoked paprika
- Pinch of red pepper flakes
- Pinch of kosher salt
- 1 tablespoon unsalted butter

Notes

....

....

....

....

....

....

Lemon Poppy Seed Granola Bars

Lunch every Wednesday in college was reserved for the Baptist Student Union. It was a great break from on-campus food, as it was all homemade, Southern and delicious. Plus, there's something about the combination of the Lord and food that just hugs you inside. Fellowship and a casserole dish simply go hand in hand. Poppy Seed Chicken was a casserole I was introduced to at the BSU and it quickly became a favorite. Though this was before I cooked, I always remember wondering, what else do you do with poppy seeds? As a chef, I learned poppy seed and lemon are a stunning combo. These granola bars are unique in flavor, good for you, and perfect to grab on-the-go during the week.

P reheat your oven to 350 degrees. On a sheet pan, toss together the oatmeal, almonds, and coconut. Bake for 8 minutes, or until light golden. Transfer to a mixing bowl and add the lemon zest, lemon juice, vanilla extract, and salt. Reduce the oven temperature to 300 degrees.

In a saucepan, bring the brown rice syrup and honey to a boil, constantly whisking for 2 minutes. Pour the mixture into the bowl with the oats and mix together completely.

Butter and line a 9-x-9-inch baking dish with parchment paper. Pour the mixture into the dish and press down with another piece of parchment paper until pressed out into an even layer. Discard the top piece of parchment paper. Sprinkle poppy seeds over the top of the mixture. Bake for about 20 to 25 minutes, or until golden. Let cool for at least 2 hours before cutting into squares.

Makes 8 to 10 bars

- 2 cups old fashioned oatmeal
- 1 cup sliced almonds
- 1 cup shredded coconut
- 3 lemons – zested, 1 – juiced
- 1 ½ teaspoons vanilla extract
- ½ teaspoon kosher salt
- ⅔ cup brown rice syrup
- ¼ cup honey
- 2 tablespoons poppy seeds

Notes

....

....

....

....

....

....

Grab 'N Go Whole-Wheat Carbonara Bites

There's a restaurant in Memphis called Bari Ristorante that Tres and I frequent. The food is authentically Italian and delightful, but the bartender, Hunter, is the real reason we go so often. He's extremely knowledgeable about Italian food and wine and we let him order for us every time. It was here that my love for Carbonara was solidified. It's one of my favorite pastas, but because it has bacon and eggs in it, I wanted to make a breakfast version. It's healthy and easy to make on a Sunday night to have on hand for a quick breakfast all week long or the perfect party bites for a weekend brunch.

Makes 24 mini frittatas

- 2 ounces whole-wheat spaghetti – broken into 1-inch pieces
- 4 slices bacon – cut into ¼-inch slices
- 4 garlic cloves – minced
- Pinch red pepper flakes
- 7 large eggs
- ½ cup freshly grated Parmesan
- ½ teaspoon kosher salt
- ¼ teaspoon freshly ground black pepper
- 1 tablespoon minced Italian parsley, plus some for garnish
- Nonstick cooking spray

Preheat your oven to 375 degrees. In a small pot of boiling salted water, cook the spaghetti until al dente. Drain and let cool. In a small skillet, fry the bacon until crispy and drain on a paper towel-lined plate. Retain 1 teaspoon of the bacon grease, turn the heat down to low, and sauté the garlic and red pepper flakes for 1 minute in the reserved bacon grease. Set aside to cool. In a large bowl, whisk together the eggs, Parmesan, salt, pepper, parsley, and garlic-pepper mixture. Spray a 24-cup muffin tin with nonstick cooking spray. Fill each cup evenly with the egg mixture, add the spaghetti pieces to each cup, then sprinkle some of the bacon on top. Bake for about 10 to 12 minutes, or until puffed and golden. Let cool slightly, then run a knife around the sides of each cup to easily remove. Garnish with parsley.

🕐 *These can be refrigerated and reheated in the microwave for up to 4 days.*

Notes

....

....

....

Mascarpone French Toast Bake

Serves 6 to 8

Tres grew up skiing and he's quite good at it. I did not grow up skiing and I'm the opposite of good at it, but it's still one of my favorite vacations. I love snow, chilly days, relaxing with a glass of wine in the hot tub, sipping coffee by the fire, cooking family-style meals for friends and family – everything about a ski vacation is cozy. On my first ski vacation with Tres and a group of friends, I made this dish and it's become a breakfast staple when cooking for a group. It can be prepped the night before and refrigerated to throw in the oven first thing in the morning – perfect before hitting the slopes or getting a good day started.

In a large bowl, beat together the eggs, milk, cream, sugar, cinnamon, nutmeg, vanilla, and salt until smooth. Set aside.

In a medium bowl, combine the mascarpone, butter, honey, sugar, and cinnamon until smooth. Open the crescent roll cans and separate each dough piece from each other. Fill each piece of crescent dough with a large dollop of the mascarpone mixture and roll the dough up. Line the rolls in a greased 9-x-13-inch baking dish, side by side.

Pour the egg mixture over the crescent rolls.

🕐 *At this point, you can refrigerate for several hours or overnight.*

When ready to bake, preheat your oven to 350 degrees. In a small bowl, mix together the pecans, brown sugar, and candied ginger. Sprinkle the nut mixture over the top of the crescent rolls. Bake for 40 to 45 minutes, or until puffed and golden.

Notes

CUSTARD:
- 8 large eggs
- 1 cup whole milk
- ½ cup heavy cream
- 2 tablespoons granulated sugar
- 2 teaspoons ground cinnamon
- ¼ teaspoon freshly grated nutmeg
- 1 teaspoon vanilla extract
- Dash kosher salt

FILLING:
- 1 (8-ounce) container mascarpone cheese – room temperature
- 4 tablespoons unsalted butter - room temperature, plus more for greasing
- ¼ cup honey
- 2 teaspoons granulated sugar
- 1 tablespoon ground cinnamon
- 3 (8 ounce) cans crescent rolls

TOPPING:
- 1 cup pecans - chopped
- ¼ cup light brown sugar
- 2 tablespoons candied ginger – minced

Best Scrambled Eggs of Your Life

The first time I ate fresh chicken eggs right from a farm, my appreciation of eggs was elevated to a new level. There is truly nothing like fresh chicken eggs – they're creamy, fluffy, rich and indulgent. I've begged Tres for years to build a chicken coop and let me raise fresh chickens, but he hasn't given in yet. For now, I'll just get my eggs at the farmer's market. I highly recommend making these scrambled eggs with fresh eggs. If you can't find them, buy good-quality eggs from the store.

In a nonstick pan, heat the butter over low heat. In a large bowl, beat together the eggs and heavy cream with a fork for several minutes until the eggs are well combined, frothy, and light yellow in color.

Pour the eggs into pan and sprinkle with about ½ teaspoon salt and ¼ teaspoon pepper. As the eggs cook, gather the cooked eggs from the sides with a silicone spatula and push into the middle of the pan. Let them cook low and slow like this, continuing to push the cooked eggs into the middle of the pan, until they're cooked and fluffy but still creamy. Plate and sprinkle liberally with Parmesan cheese and fresh herbs.

Notes

....

....

....

Serves 4

- 2 tablespoons unsalted butter
- 8 large eggs
- 2 tablespoons heavy cream
- Kosher salt and freshly ground black pepper
- Freshly grated Parmesan
- 1 tablespoon fresh basil or parsley - minced

📌 *The best-quality eggs have a dark yellow yolk.*

Fluffy Biscuits and Chocolate Gravy

You know you're starting to age when you can remember someone as a little girl and now they're a wife, a mother of two babies, a friend and someone you're excited to see living a full, happy, successful life. I met the photographer of this book, Nicole Cole, when I was in high school and her mom was my cheerleading sponsor. We would go to Mrs. Vinson's house often to prep for spirit events and homecoming and I remember Nicole – just a wee gal – running around. Nicole and I caught up post-college through our blogs and social media and since the day she started her photography business, I have been in awe of her work. Her photographs are absolutely beautiful and to see her business grow into such a success has been an inspiration. When I decided to write a cookbook, I didn't even hesitate. I knew I wanted her to photograph my food from day one. Throughout the cookbook journey, she has captured the food and meaning and has been enormously supportive of *Andrea's Cooktales* in the most perfect way, and I'm forever grateful for that and the work she's put into this book. This recipe came from her Meme, a true Southern lady. As a Christmas tradition, her mom made it for the family every year, and Nicole has kept the tradition alive with her husband and kids.

Make the gravy. In a medium saucepan set over medium-high heat, whisk together the sugar, cocoa powder, and hot water until creamed together. Add the milk and butter and bring to a boil, stirring constantly for 8 to 10 minutes, until desired thickness. Keep warm.

Make the biscuits. Preheat your oven to 425 degrees. In a large bowl, whisk together the flour, baking powder, salt, sugar, and baking soda until combined. Using a cheese grater, grate the cold butter. Add the butter to the flour mixture, tossing together quickly with your hands until it looks like cornmeal, being careful to keep the butter cold and not to handle the mixture too much. Make a well in the center of the mixture, and slowly add the milk, combining the flour and the milk with your hands lightly until the flour is absorbed but not too wet. If needed, add more milk for the mixture to come together into a ball.

Flour a clean work surface and dump the dough onto the floured surface. Pat the dough down into a flat rectangular shape, about 1 inch thick. Lift up the right and left sides of the rectangle, using both hands, and fold each flap into the center, like a book. Turn, pat the dough down, 1 inch thick again, and repeat the book fold. Pat down one last time, 1 inch thick, then using a rolling pin, smooth out the top. Using a large, round biscuit cutter, cut the dough into circles.

Brush the bottom and sides of a cast iron skillet with a little of the melted butter. Nestle the biscuits in the pan right next to each other. If there are any gaps between the biscuits, add the scraps, tearing to fit each gap. Brush with some of the melted butter and bake for 12 to 15 minutes, or until golden. Brush with the remaining melted butter and lightly sprinkle with fleur de sel. Serve with the chocolate gravy.

Makes 8 to 10 biscuits

GRAVY:

- 1 cup granulated sugar
- 3 tablespoons cocoa powder
- 2 to 3 tablespoons hot water
- ¾ cup whole milk
- 2 tablespoons unsalted butter

BISCUITS:

- 3 cups all-purpose flour
- 2 tablespoons baking powder
- 2 teaspoons kosher salt
- 1 ½ teaspoons granulated sugar
- ½ teaspoon baking soda
- 1 ½ sticks cold unsalted butter, plus ½ stick melted
- 1 cup whole milk, plus more if needed
- Fleur de sel (or flaky sea salt)

Notes

Sweet Potato and Calabrian Chile Quiche

Serves 8

More times than I can count in my cooking classes, I've gotten the question, "What's the difference between a frittata and a quiche?" The simple answer is, a quiche has crust (and is French) and a frittata doesn't have crust (and is Italian). They're technically made the same - both with eggs, cream or milk, cheese and sometimes with meat and/or veggies thrown in before being popped in the oven. I always explain them like this: it's a blank slate of eggs you can do anything with – just think pizza but with eggs. I love playing with unique ingredients for both quiche and frittata. And the best part about them? They're perfect for breakfast, lunch or dinner! This one has a unique spice that's mellowed out from the sweetness of the potato and the creaminess from the cheese.

- 2 cups peeled and diced sweet potato
- 2 tablespoons olive oil
- Kosher salt and freshly ground black pepper
- ½ cup diced onion
- 3 garlic cloves – minced
- 1 tablespoon minced rosemary
- 1 teaspoon smoked paprika
- 8 large eggs
- ¼ cup half-and-half
- 2 ounces Calabrian Chile peppers – chopped
- 4 ounces goat cheese – crumbled
- 1 refrigerated (9-inch deep dish) pie crust

Preheat your oven to 400 degrees. Spread the sweet potatoes out on a baking sheet and toss with 1 tablespoon olive oil, 1 teaspoon salt, and ½ teaspoon pepper. Roast for 15 minutes, or until soft. Remove from the oven. Turn your oven temperature down to 350 degrees.

Heat the remaining tablespoon of olive oil in a large sauté pan. Sauté the onions with ½ teaspoon salt and ¼ teaspoon pepper until soft. Add the garlic, rosemary, and smoked paprika and sauté for another minute. Turn off the heat.

Crack the eggs into a medium bowl. Add the half-and-half and beat the mixture together until smooth and fluffy. Add the roasted sweet potatoes, the onion mixture, peppers, and goat cheese. Stir to combine. Press the refrigerated pie crust into a glass or ceramic pie dish. Pour the mixture into the pie crust. Bake for 40 to 50 minutes, or until cooked through, golden, and bubbly. Cut into 8 even slices.

Notes

Calabrian Chile peppers can be found in the Italian aisle of the grocery store.

Reminisce & Relish
Your Keepsake Recipes

Foreshadowing
LUNCH

"Don't cook on the stove, Tweety Pie."

My late father was as Southern as they come. He grew up in Coldwater, Mississippi – a tiny town about thirty miles south of Memphis – and because he was country-boy to the core, he was nicknamed Coldwater by his friends. The fondest memories I have of my dad revolve around his humor. He was the king of "Southernisms" (funny phrases said by Southerners). He always spat off the funniest sayings and he had one for every situation. A few I remember: "He's enough to make a preacher cuss." "I'm gonna jerk a knot in you." "It's colder than a well digger's butt in here." "I wouldn't pee on him if he was on fire." And the list goes on. My personal favorites were also his nicknames. He called me Tweety Pie and my brother and I were both referred to as Butter Bean Butt – because we were so little.

As much as I adore cooking now, I didn't grow up in the kitchen. My neat-freak Mama knew she would be the one cleaning if my brother and I cooked and my dad was terrified we were going to burn the house down. Even when we got old enough to stay home alone, the last thing my dad would say every time he left was, "Don't cook on the stove." Since the microwave was the only kitchen device we were allowed to use, my brother and I got creative if we wanted to stay home during the lunch hour. Our favorite creations – as revolting as it may sound now – came from canned chili. Chili over white bread was our favorite and because I always loved Chili 5-Way, I would use leftover noodles to make several different versions. I recall breaking the rules a handful of times and using the stovetop because we loved making cheese quesadillas. We would pull the pan out, butter it up, brown the cheese stuffed tortillas and eat them as quick as we could so we didn't get caught. At that time in my life, I had no idea I would become a chef, but as I look back on those days of casual cooking, I think it was meant to be all along – canned chili and all. Thank goodness I'm a much better cook now and that these lunch recipes are not out of a can.

BLGGT – Bacon, Lettuce, and Grilled Green Tomato Sandwich

Serves 4

It was a blessing to know my great-grandmother, Grams, as she was alive until right before my teen years. We would take weekend trips on occasion to visit her in Coffeeville, Mississippi, a one-stoplight town – "no bigger than a minute," as she would say. What I remember about visiting her is she would always make tomato sandwiches for lunch. I didn't like them as a kid, but I have grown to love a BLT more than life itself and when I eat one, it reminds me of her. My BLT has a unique spin to it – grilled green tomatoes. This recipe is for my Grams who was always an absolute hoot to be around. We miss her all the time.

Fry or bake the bacon until crisp. Set aside on a paper towel-lined plate to drain. Heat a grill pan over high heat. Brush the sliced green tomatoes with olive oil and sprinkle with salt and pepper on both sides. Grill 2 to 3 minutes on each side, until charred with grill marks. Set aside. Spread each side of bread thinly with the softened butter and grill on each side for about 2 minutes, or until toasted with grill marks. Set aside.

In a small bowl, combine the mayonnaise, minced herbs, lemon juice, and a dash of salt and pepper. Lightly salt and pepper both sides of the heirloom tomatoes. Build the sandwiches by spreading the mayonnaise mixture on one side of each slice of bread, then place one lettuce leaf, two heirloom tomatoes, two grilled green tomatoes, and two slices of bacon on four slices of the bread. Close the sandwich with the other four slices and serve.

- 8 slices thick-cut bacon
- 2 green tomatoes - cut into 8 (¼-inch) slices
- Olive oil
- Kosher salt and freshly ground black pepper
- 1 loaf country bread - cut into 8 thick slices
- 4 tablespoons unsalted butter – softened
- ½ cup mayonnaise
- ½ cup finely minced herbs (basil, parsley, chives)
- ½ lemon - juiced
- 2 heirloom tomatoes - cut into 8 (¼-inch) slices
- 4 large lettuce leaves

Notes

Pork Rind BBQ Nachos

Living in Memphis, it's all about Memphis Grizzlies basketball in the winter and Memphis Redbirds baseball in the summer. Going to games has always been one of Tres's and my favorite weeknight outings. Of course, we love the games, but our joke is we go for the nachos. BBQ nachos are a staple in Memphis. You can get them just about anywhere, but something about watching a game with a beer and a big pile of nachos topped with BBQ is just perfection. One summer when I was on a health kick, I discovered a way to not only make them at home but cut the carbs – replace the chips with pork rinds. Buy pulled pork from your favorite barbeque restaurant or in the freezer section of the grocery store, and you have yourself a simple, delicious meal or snack.

S pread the pork rinds out on a large platter. Top the rinds evenly with the pulled pork. Sprinkle the cheese and drizzle the BBQ sauce evenly over the top – you can add as much or little of these as you like. If you like a little spice, add the sliced jalapeños. Serve family-style immediately so the rinds stay crispy.

Notes

Serves 4 to 6

- 2 (5-ounce) bags BBQ Pork Rinds
- 6 cups your favorite local pulled pork – warmed
- 8 ounces grated cheddar cheese
- 1 cup good-quality, store-bought BBQ sauce
- 2 jalapeños - sliced into rounds (optional)

Truffle Sliders

Chicago is my favorite food city in the country. Since Tres and I discovered how much we love the food scene, we try to visit once a year just to eat our faces off for a few days. It was on our first trip we discovered Truffle Sliders at a restaurant near our hotel. We loved them so much, we stopped in every night to get the sliders as a starter before our dinner reservation elsewhere. I couldn't get home fast enough to re-create them. I'm glad I did because when we went back the next year, the restaurant had changed their menu – the sliders were history. But lucky for me and Tres (and you) they've been reborn.

Make the caramelized onions. In a large sauté pan, heat the olive oil and butter over medium-low heat. Add the onions, balsamic vinegar, 1 teaspoon salt, and ½ teaspoon pepper. Let cook for 20 to 30 minutes, stirring occasionally, or until caramelized.

🕐 *Set aside and keep warm or refrigerate for up to 2 days and reheat.*

Make the sliders. Heat a grill or grill pan over medium-high heat. In a medium bowl, place the ground chuck, 2 ounces of truffle butter, 1 teaspoon salt, and ½ teaspoon pepper. Mix the ingredients together lightly with a fork, being careful not to over-mix so the meat doesn't get tough. Using a ¼ cup measuring cup, shape the meat into 10 patties. In the center of each patty, make an indention with your thumb - this will keep the sliders from puffing up when grilling.

In a small bowl, combine the remaining truffle butter with the tablespoon of honey. Open each burger bun and spread the mixture on the inside of each bun. Place the buns on the grill, cut side down, and toast for about 1 minute, then set aside on a plate. Grill the sliders for about 2 minutes on each side. When you flip the burgers, top each one with a slice of cheese and close the grill lid for the last minute. In another small bowl, combine mayonnaise, truffle oil, and the teaspoon of honey. Build the sliders by spreading the mayonnaise mixture on the inside of the buns. Top with a cheesy burger and the caramelized onions.

Makes 10 sliders

- 2 tablespoons olive oil
- 2 tablespoons unsalted butter
- 2 onions - sliced thin
- 1 tablespoon balsamic vinegar
- Kosher salt and freshly ground black pepper
- 1 pound ground chuck (80 lean/20 fat)
- 3 ounces truffle butter - room temperature
- 1 tablespoon plus 1 teaspoon honey
- 10 mini burger buns or rolls
- 4 ounces Havarti cheese
- ¼ cup mayonnaise
- 1 teaspoon truffle oil

Notes

....

....

....

....

....

....

Herb Mustard Chicken Salad

Serves 6 to 8

People tell me all the time that they hate mayonnaise. I immediately ask them if they know what's in it. They're typically surprised to hear that it's made up of some of their favorite ingredients: egg, olive oil, lemon juice and Dijon mustard. I happen to love all those ingredients too, but I'll be honest, even though I know what's in mayonnaise and like it, globs of the white stuff have never been my favorite. I often leave it off my sandwiches unless it's a flavored version and anything with mayonnaise as one of the main ingredients, I skip. That being said, I have never liked chicken salad very much, until I made this clean, fresh, herb-flavored one. It's a spin on the traditional chicken salad but mayo-free and healthier. This is a winner for both mayo and non-mayo fans alike!

Make the dressing. Combine the white balsamic reduction, whole grain mustard, Dijonnaise, lemon juice, garlic, Italian seasoning, a dash of salt and pepper, and olive oil by whisking in a small bowl or shaking in a Mason jar.

Make the salad. Preheat your oven to 425 degrees. On a baking sheet, toss the chicken tenderloins together with the olive oil and a heavy sprinkle of salt and pepper. Roast for 15 to 20 minutes, or until cooked through. Set aside to cool. When cooled, dice the chicken tenders into small cubes and place in a large bowl. Add the celery, basil, chives, dill, parsley, and the dressing. Toss together until all the chicken is coated in the dressing and herbs. Taste for seasoning and add more salt and pepper if needed. Serve with grilled bread and lettuce cups.

🍴 *Refrigerating the salad before serving enhances the flavor. It can be made ahead and refrigerated in an air-tight container for up to 3 days.*

DRESSING:

- ¼ cup white balsamic reduction
- ¼ cup whole grain mustard
- 3 tablespoons Dijonnaise
- 1 lemon – juiced
- 2 garlic cloves – minced
- 2 teaspoons Italian seasoning
- Kosher salt and freshly ground black pepper
- ½ cup extra virgin olive oil

SALAD:

- 2 ½ pounds chicken tenderloins
- 2 tablespoons olive oil
- Kosher salt and freshly ground black pepper
- 1 cup chopped celery
- ¼ cup minced fresh basil
- ¼ cup sliced fresh chives
- 2 tablespoons minced fresh dill
- 1 tablespoon minced fresh parsley
- Grilled bread – for serving
- Lettuce cups – for serving

Notes

....

....

....

....

....

Sweet 'N Salty Pizza Duo

2 medium pizzas
Serves 4 to 6

As a kid, there's nothing more exciting on a Friday or Saturday night than your parents asking the question, "Do you want to order a pizza?" Throw that in with, "Let's rent a movie," and you're tickled pink – at least I always was. Pizza nights are a bit different for me now, but they're just as grand. The old-school me loved a good ole fashioned pepperoni delivery with a Dr. Pepper on the side. The adult-me likes a homemade creation with unique ingredients and a side of red wine. These two pizzas are my favorite to make when having a group of friends over for game night – each unique in flavor; both salty, sweet and a huge hit with a crowd. P.S. Sometimes I still like a pepperoni delivery – but with wine.

In a measuring cup or bowl, combine the wine and 1 cup water. Heat in the microwave until warm – 100 to 110 degrees. Pour into a stand mixer with the yeast, honey, salt, and 3 tablespoons of the olive oil. Stir with your hands to combine. With a dough hook attached, begin mixing at medium-high speed, slowly adding 1 cup of flour at a time until the dough begins to form and is slightly sticky. If it's too sticky, add more flour. If you don't have a stand mixer, do it manually by putting the wet ingredients into a bowl and slowly incorporating the flour with a wooden spoon until it all comes together.

On a well-floured surface, bring dough together in a ball and knead for about 3 to 4 minutes, or until smooth and elastic, adding flour to the board if it sticks. Pour the remaining 1 tablespoon of olive oil into a bowl and spread around so it coats the inside of the bowl. Place the ball of dough in the bowl and roll around, covering in olive oil.

🕐 **_Cover with plastic wrap and refrigerate until ready to use – up to several days._**

When ready to use, flour your board again so the dough doesn't stick. Cut the dough into two even pieces. One at a time, using a rolling pin, roll each piece out into an oval/rectangle shape and place on an oiled baking sheet. Get ready to build your pizzas.

QUICK PIZZA DOUGH:

- ¼ cup dry white wine
- 2 packages of pizza crust yeast (no rise necessary)
- 1 tablespoon honey
- 1 teaspoon kosher salt
- 4 tablespoons olive oil
- 3 ½ cups all-purpose flour, plus more for kneading

Notes

📌 _You can prep the ingredients for each pizza several hours ahead. Set them aside in bowls or on plates so they're ready to go when you roll your dough out. If dough sits in open air too long, it can become dry and crack._

Fig, Ricotta, & Prosciutto Pizza:

• ¼ cup good-quality extra virgin olive oil
• 6 ounces fresh mozzarella – sliced thin
• 4 ounces ricotta
• 10 to 12 dry black mission figs – sliced
• 3 to 4 ounces prosciutto – chopped

Preheat your oven to 475 degrees. Brush the olive oil evenly over prepared pizza dough. Top with the mozzarella, dollops of ricotta, figs, and prosciutto. Bake for 10-to 12 minutes, or until crust is golden and crispy.

Apple, Smoked Gouda, & Bacon Pizza:

• ¼ cup good-quality extra virgin olive oil
• 2 shallots – sliced thin
• Kosher salt
• 8 ounces smoked Gouda – grated
• 1 small Granny Smith Apple – sliced thin
• 5 slices bacon – fried and crumbled

Preheat your oven to 475 degrees. In a small sauté pan, heat the olive oil over medium heat. Sauté the shallots with a sprinkle of salt until soft. Pour the olive oil mixture over prepared pizza dough and spread evenly. Top with the smoked Gouda, apples, and bacon. Bake for 10 to 12 minutes, or until crust is golden and crispy.

Southern Ceviche

I'm the opposite of a picky eater. I will literally try – and typically like – anything. People are always shocked to find out that I used to be the pickiest eater in the world. In our first week of dating, I actually spit an eel sushi roll into a napkin right in front of Tres because it grossed me out so badly. I hardly knew the guy and I was spitting my food into a napkin – it's a wonder he didn't leave right then and there. Luckily, he stuck with me, as it's because of him I'm not a picky eater anymore and seafood is now one of my favorite foods. I always encourage picky eaters to simply TRY food before deciding not to like it. Ceviche is one of those things. If you have never had it, imagine clean, fresh, citrusy flavor – plus, my version is a little Southern.

Make the tortilla chips. Preheat your oven to 375 degrees. Line a baking sheet with foil. Spread the tortilla triangles on the baking sheet, brush each side with olive oil, and sprinkle the tops with salt. Bake for about 10 to 12 minutes, rotating the pan once, until light brown and crispy. Set aside until ready to serve.
🕐 *Can be stored in an air-tight container for up to 4 days.*

Make the ceviche. Bring a medium saucepan halfway filled with water to a simmer. When it starts to bubble, add the calamari slices. Let poach for about one minute then add the shrimp. Let the shrimp poach for about 30 seconds, or until they just turn a very light pink. Drain, rinse, and pat the seafood dry.

Place the calamari and shrimp in a large bowl with the cubed fish, lime zest and juice, lemon zest and juice, orange zest and juice, black-eyed peas, bell pepper, serrano pepper, jalapeño, green onions, cilantro, and about 1 teaspoon of salt.
🕐 *Stir together until all the seafood is coated with the juice. Cover and put in the refrigerator for at least 3 hours or overnight.*
When the ceviche is ready, the fish will be transparent. If you desire, stir in cubed avocado before serving. Spoon into decorative glasses or bowls and garnish with homemade chips.

Serves 4

- 4 corn tortillas - cut into eighths
- Olive oil
- Kosher salt
- ½ pound calamari tubes - thinly sliced
- ½ pound peeled and deveined shrimp - tails off and cut into thirds
- ½ pound white fish (tilapia, cod, snapper) - cut into small cubes
- 2 limes - zest of one, juice of both
- 2 lemons - zest of one, juice of both
- 2 oranges - zest of one, juice of both
- 1 (15-ounce) can black-eyed peas - drained and rinsed
- ½ cup minced (yellow or orange) bell pepper
- 2 serrano chili peppers - seeded and minced
- 1 jalapeño pepper - seeded and minced
- 4 green onions – thinly sliced
- 2 tablespoons minced cilantro
- 1 avocado - cubed (optional)

Notes

....

....

....

....

Perfect Lobster Rolls

Makes 8 rolls

I'm a serious "When in Rome," traveler when it comes to food. Whatever you're supposed to eat in a city, I get obsessed with while there and eat it the entire time. When Tres and I visited Maine, Cape Cod, Salem, and Boston for a New England adventure the week of our first anniversary, I become obsessed with eating lobster rolls and had one everywhere we went. I researched how to make authentic ones and discovered two musts: homemade mayonnaise and live lobsters. Boiling live lobsters may disturb you at first, but it's easier than you think and after you taste the difference in the meat, you'll never go back.

Make the mayonnaise. In a stand mixer with a whisk attachment or a food processor, combine the egg yolks, lemon juice, vinegar, Dijon mustard, salt, and sugar until smooth. With the machine running on high speed, stream the oil into the mixture very slowly – it should become thick and light in color. This takes time, but it's worth it in the end.

🕐 *When the mayo comes together, spoon it into a container or jar and refrigerate until ready to use - up to one week.*

Make the lobster rolls. In a large bowl, combine the lobster meat, ½ cup homemade mayonnaise, celery, chives, dill, and salt. Taste for seasoning, and add more salt or mayonnaise if needed. Heat a grill pan to high heat. Brush the inside of the hot dog buns generously with the melted butter. Place on the grill cut side down for about 1 to 2 minutes, or until charred. Fill each bun with the lobster mixture. Top with extra chives.

HOMEMADE MAYONNAISE:

- 2 egg yolks
- 1 tablespoon lemon juice
- 2 tablespoons red wine vinegar
- 1 tablespoon Dijon mustard
- Dash of kosher salt
- Dash of granulated sugar
- 1 cup vegetable oil

ROLLS:

- 3 (1 to 1 ½-pound) whole, cooked lobsters – meat removed from tails and claws and chopped into large pieces
- ½ cup homemade mayonnaise, plus more to preference
- 3 stalks celery – diced small
- 2 tablespoons fresh chives – sliced, plus extra for garnish
- 1 tablespoon fresh dill – minced
- 1 teaspoon kosher salt
- 8 hot dog buns
- ½ cup unsalted butter – melted

Notes

....

....

....

....

📌 *To boil live lobsters: Heat a large pot of water over high heat. When the water comes to a rapid boil, add the lobsters, head first. Boil for about 12 minutes (for 1-pound lobsters) and about 15 minutes (for 1 ½-pound lobsters). Remove and let cool.*

Corn Salad with Roasted Shrimp

Serves 6 to 8

Everyone needs a go-to picnic dish and this one has been mine for years. It reminds me of the Fourth of July picnics I used to go on with my parents when we were kids – blanket laid out, sun shining down and a firework show at night. The sweet corn makes this salad light and summery and the cilantro-jalapeño vinaigrette gives it Southwestern flair. It's a serious crowd pleaser – my friends and family flip out over this dish.

Make the salad: Preheat your oven to 400 degrees. On a sheet pan, toss together the shrimp, olive oil, and a heavy sprinkle of salt and pepper. Roast for about 8 minutes, or until shrimp just turn pink. Set aside to cool.

Heat a grill pan over high heat. Place the corn on the grill and turn every few minutes for about 12 minutes, or until corn has several charred pieces. Set the corn aside to cool slightly but is still warm. When cool enough to handle, take the corn kernels off the cob, slicing downward with a sharp knife directly into a large bowl. To the bowl of corn, add the butter, green onions, avocado cubes, and about 1 teaspoon salt, and ¼ teaspoon pepper. Stir to combine until the butter is melted.

Make the dressing. In a small bowl, combine the cilantro, jalapeño, vinegar, lime juice, agave, salt, and pepper. Slowly whisk in the extra virgin olive oil until the dressing comes together.

Assemble the salad. Pour the dressing over the corn salad and toss together. Toss the shrimp into the salad or place on top. Refrigerate until ready to serve. For a great side dish, the shrimp can be omitted.

SALAD:
- 1 pound uncooked shrimp – peeled and deveined
- 1 tablespoon olive oil
- Kosher salt and freshly ground black pepper
- 6 large ears of corn – shucked
- 2 tablespoons unsalted butter
- 6 green onions – sliced thin
- 1 large avocado – cubed

DRESSING:
- 1 cup cilantro – chopped
- 2 tablespoons seeded, minced jalapeño
- 2 tablespoons white wine vinegar
- 1 lime – juiced
- 3 tablespoons agave nectar
- 1 teaspoon kosher salt
- ½ teaspoon freshly ground black pepper
- ½ cup good-quality extra virgin olive oil

Notes

Slawsa Dog with Caramelized Apples and Onions

In both undergraduate and graduate journalism school, my focus was broadcasting. I wasn't sure if I would ever go into that exact field, but sometimes life takes turns and what you're meant to do ends up finding you, even if you're not trying to make it happen. When I started my blog, I partnered with Slawsa, the most delicious condiment I have ever eaten. Julie Busha, founder and CEO of Slawsa, is best known for pitching her up-and-coming product on the well-known TV show *Shark Tank*. Ever since, Slawsa has blown up and can be found in grocery stores all over the country. When she contacted me to create a recipe with Slawsa and go on a local morning show to talk about the product, I got the chance to dust off my broadcasting boots. Eventually, I became a regular contributor to the morning show and that led to other opportunities such as judging the Memphis edition of *Big BBQ Brawl* on the *Cooking Channel*. Julie is a fantastic, inspiring entrepreneur who I keep in touch with and have looked up to through the startup of my business. It was also because of her I got my feet wet again in broadcasting. Y'all can thank her for this recipe: it's the one I featured on the morning show and the first recipe I ever created with Slawsa. Now, I put Slawsa on everything!

eat the butter over medium heat. Add the onions and the apples. Season with a dash of salt and pepper. Let the mixture cook until slightly golden, stirring occasionally. Add the zest and juice from the orange, brown sugar, and crystallized ginger. Cook until browned and caramelized, stirring occasionally, about 15 minutes. Add salt to taste.

🕐 *Keep warm over low heat or refrigerate for up to 2 days and reheat.*

In a Dutch oven or pot over medium-high heat, combine the beer, salt, peppercorns, thyme, and bratwurst. Let the ingredients slightly come to a boil for about one minute then immediately lower the heat to a simmer. Cover the pot and let the brats braise for about 10 to 12 minutes.

Heat a grill or grill pan over high heat. Take the brats out of the liquid, place on paper towels, and lightly pat dry. Brush the brats evenly with olive oil on all sides. Cook on the grill for about 6 to 8 minutes, turning every couple of minutes, until all sides are charred, crispy, and cooked through.

Open the buns and toast the insides, face down on the grill, for about 2 minutes, or until charred with grill marks. Serve the brats inside the buns, top with the caramelized apple-onion mixture and a generous scoop of Slawsa.

Notes

....

....

....

Serves 4

TOPPING:
- 2 tablespoons unsalted butter
- 1 yellow onion - thinly sliced
- 1 Granny Smith apple - thinly sliced
- Kosher salt and freshly ground black pepper
- 1 orange – zested and juiced
- 2 tablespoons light brown sugar
- 1 tablespoon crystallized ginger - minced

DOG:
- 2 (12-ounce) bottles Hefeweizen beer
- 2 teaspoons kosher salt
- 1 teaspoon peppercorns
- 1 small bunch of fresh thyme
- 4 uncooked bratwurst
- Olive Oil
- 4 pretzel buns (or your favorite brat bun)
- Slawsa - for the perfect topping

South in Your Mouth Burger

My parents grilled outdoors every Sunday – it was an unwritten family tradition. The food they chose to cook out would vary from week to week, but I remember having burgers regularly. As kids, my brother and I ate our burgers plain. I have no idea what we were thinking eating meat and bread alone, but I'm guessing it's because we had never had a South in your Mouth Burger. This burger creation is topped with every Southern ingredient I could think of that made sense, and it's the best burger I've ever cooked.

Make the pimento cheese (page 78) and refrigerate until ready to use. Make the bacon. Preheat your oven to 375 degrees. Lay the bacon slices flat on a baking sheet lined with parchment paper. Bake for 12 to 15 minutes. In a small bowl, combine the honey and bourbon. Heat in the microwave for about 10 seconds. Brush the mixture onto the bacon slices and place them back in the oven for another 3 to 5 minutes, or until crisp. Set aside.

Make the green tomatoes. In a sauté pan, heat the oil over medium heat. Cut the tomato into four slices and salt and pepper both sides. Combine the flour and cornmeal in a shallow bowl. Beat the egg in a separate shallow bowl. Lightly dip each tomato into the flour mixture, then into the egg mixture, then back into the flour mixture. Fry the tomatoes for 2 to 3 minutes on each side, or until golden. Set aside.

Cook the burgers. Heat a grill to high heat. Grill the inside of the burger buns for about 1 minute, or until toasted with grill marks. Set aside. Form 4 thick patties with the meat. Brush both sides with olive oil and salt and pepper liberally. Before grilling, make an indention in the middle of each patty with your thumb - this will keep meat from puffing up when grilling. Grill for about 4 minutes on each side for medium-rare. Refrain from pressing down with spatula when cooking – that removes the juiciness from the burger.

Build the burgers. Spread pimento cheese on both sides of the burger buns. Place the burger patties on the bottom half of the buns, top with the green tomatoes, split each bacon slice in half, then top with bacon slices, and close with the bun tops.

PIMENTO CHEESE:
- See page 78

HONEY BOURBON BACON:
- 4 slices thick-cut bacon
- 1 tablespoon honey
- ½ tablespoon bourbon

PAN SEARED GREEN TOMATOES:
- ¼ cup vegetable oil, for frying
- 1 large green tomato
- Kosher salt and freshly ground black pepper
- ¼ cup all-purpose flour
- ¼ cup cornmeal
- 1 large egg

BURGERS:
- 4 Hawaiian Bun or Brioche Rolls – split
- 1 pound ground chuck (80/20)
- 1 tablespoon olive oil
- Kosher salt and freshly ground black pepper

Notes

Barbie Caico e Pepe

On a trip to Rome a few years ago, it didn't take long for my best friend and I to discover the traditional Roman dish, Caico e Pepe, to be one of our favorite pasta dishes of all time. Coming from two pasta-obsessed, self-proclaimed pasta connoisseurs, you can imagine Caico e Pepe is no joke. It's truly one of the best pasta dishes ever. And the best part? It only has three main ingredients – spaghetti, cheese, and pepper. After many trips down the spice aisle eyeing beautiful pink peppercorns and wondering what to do with them, I decided to try them in Cacio e Pepe. The flavor of pink peppercorns is somewhat floral and sweet. They've become a staple in my kitchen, but I love them most as a fun addition to this traditional pepper pasta. The light, somewhat fruity flavor that comes from the bright burst of pink in this dish makes it so unique. It's like Chef Barbie sprinkled dust all over the top!

Preheat your oven to 400 degrees. Line a baking sheet with a silicone mat or parchment paper. Make the Parmesan crisps by freshly grating the Parmesan cheese. Pour ¼ of the grated cheese onto the silicone mat and lightly press down. Do this three more times, making sure there's at least ½ inch between each circle, until you have four Parmesan circles. Bake for about 4 minutes, or until crisp and light golden. Let cool. Then using a spatula, lightly lift the crisps from the mat, being careful not to break them. Set aside until ready to serve.

Grate the Pecorino cheese and set aside. Bring a heavily salted pot of water to a boil. Boil the pasta a couple of minutes less than package directions, until al dente. This is very important, as the pasta needs to be cooked through but still have a firm bite. You can only get this perfect by closely watching the pasta and testing a noodle at a time until it's ready.

While the pasta is boiling, heat the butter and olive oil in a large sauté pan over medium-low heat, until melted. Add the black pepper and about ½ teaspoon salt to the pan, lightly cooking together for about one minute. Using a ladle, add about ½ cup of pasta water from the pot to the sauté pan. When the pasta is al dente, using tongs, add it directly the sauté pan, and toss together with the pepper sauce for about one minute – keeping the pasta water in the pot. Remove the sauté pan from the heat and slowly add the Pecorino cheese, a little at a time with a little more pasta water, vigorously stirring everything together until the cheese melts and it creates a creamy sauce. Be careful to not add all the cheese at once or it will clump. Continue stirring everything together. If the sauce seems to dry, add more pasta water. Serve garnished with Parmesan crisps and sprinkled with pink peppercorns.

Serves 4

- 1 (8-ounce) block Parmesan cheese
- 1 (8-ounce) block Pecorino Romano cheese
- Kosher salt
- 1 pound good-quality spaghetti
- 4 tablespoons unsalted butter
- ¼ cup olive oil
- 3 teaspoons (or to taste) freshly ground black pepper
- 2 teaspoons (or to taste) coarsely smashed pink peppercorns

Notes

Reminisce & Relish Your Keepsake Recipes

Plot Twists
APPS & COCKTAILS

"So caught up in you, little girl."

I grew up in the 80s and 90s around good music. My parents were young, fun and took my brother and me everywhere with them – festivals, concerts and many other outdoor events surrounded by music. I recall being in the back of the car with my brother and my parents singing songs to us – my dad and mom belting out 38 Special's "Caught Up in You" then turning around and pointing at me on the "little girl," lyric. I remember the little shed in our backyard, complete with every rock instrument known to man, my dad jamming out and letting us join him. And I will never forget the old record/cassette tape player combo in our living room, always spinning records and tapes when company came to visit. It all undoubtedly had a huge impact on my brother and me, because to this day, we still rock out together over food and beer to the music we grew up with. Music may be a silly memory to relish when it comes to food, but believe it or not, it's at the center of my cooking, party planning and entertaining.

I have four rules for hosting a flawless, fun cocktail party: 1) Make both a grocery and a prep list and check off as you go. 2) Prep food ahead – you can freeze and refrigerate more than you think – then assemble, cook and bake right before the party. 3) Don't cook everything – buy a few local favorites so you're not in the kitchen all day and night. 4) Have fun when you're cooking – that's where the music comes into the picture. When you plan a cocktail party, food and drink should be the priority, but try not to forget the music in the kitchen and at the party – you'll cook a little swifter and the party will be a little more entertaining. These small bites and cocktails will get you in the party planning mood – pair an old-school playlist with each one, get in the kitchen and jam out.

Truffle Deviled Eggs with Candy Bacon

When someone tells me they're not into deviled eggs, I urge them to try this recipe because it was created for just that reason. I was never a deviled eggs fan – until these. One evening I was feeling adventurous in the kitchen and because Tres loves deviled eggs, I decided to make some that I could potentially like. I used my favorite ingredients – bacon and truffle – and instead of a huge glob of mayonnaise I created creaminess using cream cheese. These eggs are light and fluffy with a flavor combo that'll quickly change any deviled egg hater's mind.

Make the candy bacon. Preheat your oven to 350 degrees. In a small bowl, mix together the brown sugar, granulated sugar, chili powder, and cayenne. Dip each strip of bacon into the mixture, coating evenly on all sides, and place on a baking sheet lined with parchment paper. Using a spoon, spread the leftover mixture thickly and evenly over the top of each piece of bacon. Bake for 12 to 15 minutes, or until caramelized.

Make the deviled eggs. In a large pot, place the eggs and fill with water until the eggs are submerged. Place on the stove over high heat and bring to a heavy boil for one minute. Take off the heat, cover the pot, and let sit for 12 minutes. Drain the eggs and rinse with cool water. To peel, crack each egg at the top and at the bottom – these are the best places to start peeling because air pockets get into them from here – and then use your fingers and pull apart the shells. If it gets tricky, dip the egg back into cool water and continue peeling.

Cut the eggs in half longways and scoop out the yolks into a large bowl. Smash the yolks thoroughly with a fork. Add the cream cheese, sour cream, mayonnaise, truffle oil, salt, and white pepper. Whip the mixture together with a hand mixer until smooth. Transfer mixture to a piping bag, and pipe into the eggs –
🕐 *mixture can be made one day ahead and refrigerated.*
Cut the bacon into ½-inch strips and stick a piece into each egg.

Notes

....

....

....

Makes 24 eggs

BACON:
- 2 tablespoons light brown sugar
- 1 tablespoon granulated sugar
- ½ teaspoon chili powder
- ⅛ teaspoon cayenne
- 3 strips thick-cut bacon

EGGS:
- 1 dozen large eggs
- 4 ounces cream cheese – room temperature
- ¼ cup sour cream
- 2 tablespoons mayonnaise
- 2 tablespoons truffle oil
- 1 teaspoon truffle or kosher salt
- ½ teaspoon white pepper

📌 *For easy peeling, buy eggs at least one week before boiling. Older eggs peel the easiest.*

If you don't have a piping bag, use a plastic bag with a snipped corner to fill the eggs.

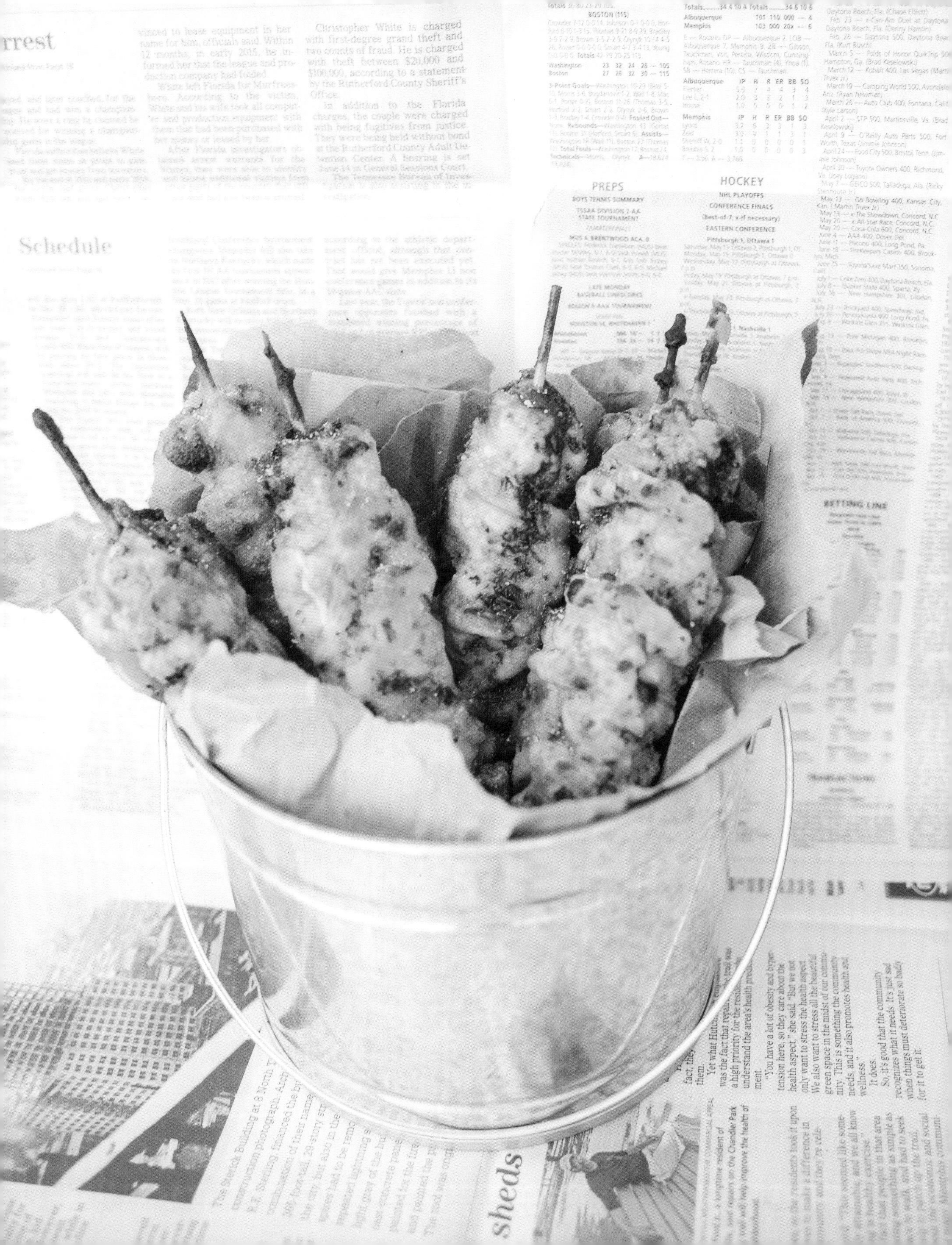
Schedule
PREPS
HOCKEY
NHL PLAYOFFS
BETTING LINE

Mississippi Gas Station Chicken-on-a-Stick

Makes 6 to 8 sticks

On my first trip to the Mississippi Delta to visit the college I would attend, I stopped at a gas station for something to drink. While I was checking out, I noticed these gigantic, glorious skewered sticks of fried chicken behind the counter. They were begging for me to try them, so I got one. That chicken on a stick changed my life. When I discovered they were in almost every gas station where the university was located, I was thrilled. Thank goodness cheerleading kept me in shape because chicken on a stick became a regular meal for me. When I started cooking, I had to re-create them. This is an easy appetizer you can make for any party or gathering. What's the secret that makes it so delicious? Pickles and a sprinkle of salt!

C ut the chicken into 1 ½ -inch cubes. Alternately thread the chicken and pickles onto wooden skewers, starting and ending with the chicken. There should be about 5 pieces of chicken and 4 to 8 pickles on each skewer. Salt and pepper the skewered chicken on all sides. Place the threaded skewers in a long, shallow bowl or baking dish and cover in the buttermilk. Cover and refrigerate for at least one hour.

In a Dutch oven or cast-iron skillet large enough to fit the skewers, heat about 2 inches of vegetable oil to 375 degrees. In a wide, shallow bowl, place 1 cup of the flour. In another wide, shallow bowl, whisk together the other cup of flour, corn starch, beer, soda water, and honey until smooth.

Working one at a time, take each skewer out of the buttermilk and let most the liquid drip off. Dip into the flour to lightly coat the chicken and pickles and then dredge in the batter. Fry the skewers in the hot oil for 6 to 8 minutes, or until golden. Fry up to three skewers at a time but no more - overcrowding will cause the oil temperature to go down. Drain the fried skewers on a baking sheet covered in paper towels. As soon as they come out of the oil, sprinkle with salt.

- 2 pounds boneless, skinless chicken breasts
- 1 (16-ounce) jar dill pickle chips
- Kosher salt and freshly ground black pepper
- 1 ½ cups buttermilk
- Vegetable oil, for frying
- 2 cups all-purpose flour
- 1 tablespoon corn starch
- ¾ cup beer
- ½ cup soda water
- 1 teaspoon honey

Notes

If skewers are too long to fit into the Dutch oven or cast-iron to fry, cut them in half.

Pimento Cheese Three Ways: Fried, Grilled, Baked

Pimento cheese makes me think of football season. Maybe because it's the perfect game day snack or maybe because it's orange: the color of Tres's alma mater, University of Tennessee. We constantly entertain during football season, and a Vols game is never missed. While I'm not big on football, I love being outdoors in the fall and especially love cooking for huge groups of people. I make this pimento cheese every football season and turn it into multiple appetizers. This recipe is the most delicious pimento cheese ever and each is easy and can be served alone or with dippers.

Easy Pimento Cheese:

4 cups – approximately

Using a handheld or stand mixer with a paddle attachment, beat together the cream cheese, smoked cheddar, pepper jack, chipotle peppers, pimentos, pickle relish, garlic powder, smoked paprika, and a dash of salt on low until the mixture is combined. Increase the speed to high, and slowly add the mayo until it's the consistency you desire. Refrigerate until ready to use.

- 8 ounces cream cheese – room temperature
- 8 ounces smoked cheddar cheese – grated
- 8 ounces pepper jack cheese – grated
- 3 chipotle peppers in adobo sauce – rinsed, patted dry, and minced
- 7 to 8 ounces pimentos – drained
- 4 teaspoons pickle relish
- ½ teaspoon garlic powder
- ½ teaspoon smoked paprika
- Kosher salt
- ¼ cup mayonnaise – plus extra if desired

Pimento cheese can be made ahead and stays fresh for up to one week.

Fried: Pimento Cheese Poppers

30 to 40 poppers

- 3 cups pimento cheese
- ¾ cup all-purpose flour
- 2 large eggs – beaten
- 2 cups panko bread crumbs
- Vegetable oil, for frying

Using a small ice cream scoop and your hands, roll the pimento cheese into 1-inch balls, and place on a baking sheet. Refrigerate for at least 30 minutes to slightly firm. In a small bowl, place the flour. In another small bowl, beat the eggs. In a third small bowl, place the panko bread crumbs.

In a Dutch oven or cast iron skillet, heat about 1 ½ inches of oil to 375 degrees. Working one at a time, dip the pimento cheese balls lightly into the flour, then the egg, and then cover well with the panko bread crumbs. Place the poppers back on the baking sheet until ready to fry. Fry five balls at a time for about 3 minutes, or until golden. Using a slotted spoon, transfer to a plate lined with paper towels to drain.

Notes

Grilled: Pimento Grilled Cheesies

20 mini sandwiches

- 20 slices of pancetta (Italian-style bacon)
- 40 slices of white bread (about 2 loaves)
- 2 cups pimento cheese
- Unsalted butter – room temperature

In a sauté pan over medium heat, fry the pancetta until extra crispy. Set aside on a paper towel-lined plate to drain. Wipe the pan out and set over medium-high heat. Using large biscuit cutters (about 4 inches in diameter), cut out one round from each slice of bread. Build the sandwiches by adding a large spoonful of the pimento cheese mixture to half the bread circles. Top each with one slice of pancetta then close the sandwiches with the remaining bread circles.

Lightly butter each side of the sandwiches and place in the sauté pan. Lightly smash the sandwiches down with a spatula as they cook. Flip after about 2 minutes, or when the bread is golden and the cheese starts to melt. Cook on the other side for another 2 minutes.

Notes

....

....

....

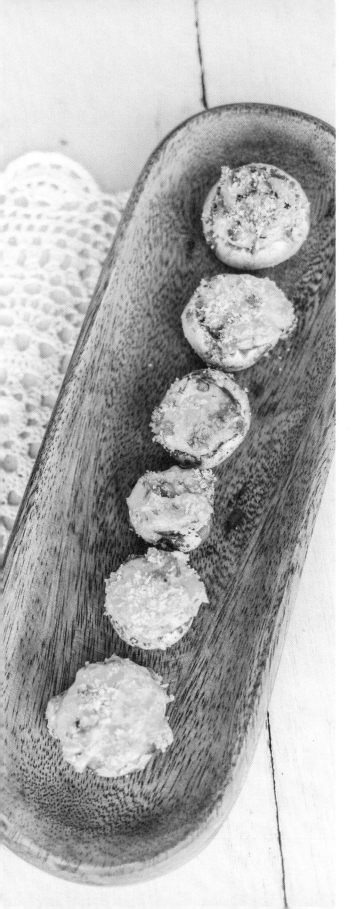

Baked: Pimento Cheese and Salami Stuffed Mushrooms

24 to 30 mushrooms

- 2 (8-ounce) packages white button mushrooms
- 1 tablespoon olive oil
- 2 tablespoons finely chopped shallots
- Kosher salt
- ½ cup finely chopped salami
- ¾ cup pimento cheese
- ½ cup panko bread crumbs

Preheat your oven to 425 degrees. Stem the mushrooms, reserve ¼ cup of the stems and chop finely. In a small sauté pan, heat the olive oil over medium-low heat. Sauté the shallots together with the stem pieces and a dash of salt for about 3 minutes, or until soft. Transfer the mixture to a medium bowl and let cool slightly. Stir in the salami and pimento cheese. Stuff the filling into mushroom crowns and sprinkle with panko bread crumbs. Place on a baking sheet lined with parchment paper and bake for 8 to 10 minutes, or until cheese is melted and tops are golden.

Notes

....

....

....

Cream Taco Dip

Serves a very large group

When I was a teenager, my brother and I went to a friend's pool party and were served Cream Taco Dip. I was so obsessed with this dip, I practically drank the entire bowl while everyone else was in the pool. I told Mama, and she got the recipe from our friend's mom. This is my version with a little spicy spin: chorizo. It can also be made without the meat for a vegetarian option.

- 1 pound chorizo
- 1 (10-ounce) can tomatoes with green chilies
- 1 (15-ounce) can chili, no beans
- 1 (15-ounce) can Ranch Style® beans
- 1 (32 ounce) package Velveeta® cheese
- 1 cup heavy whipping cream
- Tortilla chips – for serving

In a large pot or Dutch oven, cook the chorizo over medium heat until done, breaking up the meat into small pieces as it cooks. Drain the fat from the pot. Pour in the tomatoes, chili, ranch style beans, and stir together. Cube the Velveeta®, add to the pot, and stir until melted. Add the heavy whipping cream and stir to combine. Let the dip heat completely and serve warm with tortilla chips.

🕐 *Dip can be made ahead and refrigerated up to 3 days ahead or frozen up to 3 months.*

Notes

Buffalo Hot Wing Hummus

Sometimes I have a craving for something unhealthy and I just want a healthy version of it. One day I was craving fried hot wings, so I made up this hummus dip to nip it in the bud. This dip is a perfect clean-eating version of hot wings and perfect for a Super Bowl party or game day.

In a small sauté pan over medium-low heat, toast the sesame seeds until light brown. Transfer the toasted sesame seeds to a food processor, and add the olive oil. Blend until it comes together into a runny paste. To the food processor, add both the beans, some of the reserved bean liquid, lemon juice, red wine vinegar, garlic, salt, and buffalo wings sauce. Blend all the ingredients together until smooth. If it's not smooth enough, add more liquid from the beans until it's to your desired consistency. Taste for seasoning and add more salt if needed. Pour in a bowl and top with the cheese and a drizzle of the buffalo wings sauce. Serve with celery, carrots, cucumbers, or pita bread.

🕐 *Hummus can be made ahead and refrigerated for up to 4 days.*

Notes

- ⅓ cup sesame seeds
- 3 tablespoons olive oil
- 1 (15 to 16 ounce) can garbanzo beans - drained
- 1 (15 to 16 ounce) can cannellini beans - drained, ⅓ cup liquid reserved
- 1 lemon – juiced
- 2 teaspoons red wine vinegar
- 4 garlic cloves - roughly chopped
- 1 ½ teaspoons kosher salt, plus more to taste
- ⅓ cup Frank's RedHot® Buffalo Wings Sauce, plus extra for drizzling
- ¼ cup blue, gorgonzola, or feta cheese
- Celery, carrots, cucumbers, or pita bread – for serving

Fried Green Tomatoes with Herb Goat Cheese

Serves 4 to 6

Little did I know, I would make my lifelong girlfriends in college. Over ten years out of college and I still talk to my college friends every week – we call it the group text that never ends. When I have a problem or need advice, they are always a part of the equation that solves it. And since we don't all live in the same city, we try to get together at least once a year. I see this continuing for the rest of our lives, and I know they're the ones, along with Tres, with whom I will grow old and grey. For some reason, fried green tomatoes make me think of them. Maybe it's because of the movie or maybe because these tomatoes were a regular menu item when we all lived together in the Delta, but these "tomaters" are for them.

Make the herb goat cheese. In a small bowl, mix together the goat cheese, lemon juice, basil, chives, and a dash of salt and pepper. *Set aside or refrigerate until ready to use – up to one week.*

Make the fried green tomatoes. In a cast iron skillet or Dutch oven, heat 1 inch of vegetable oil to 350 degrees. In a medium bowl, whisk together the flour and buttermilk until smooth. In a shallow bowl, mix together the cornmeal, garlic powder, paprika, and cayenne. Slice the tomatoes into ½-inch thick slices. Salt and pepper the tomato slices on both sides, dip in the buttermilk mixture, and then coat in the cornmeal mixture. Fry about 4 minutes, or until golden brown. Using a slotted spoon, transfer to a paper towel-lined plate to drain and sprinkle with salt when they come out of the oil. Plate the tomatoes and top with a dollop of the herb goat cheese. Serve warm or at room temperature.

- Vegetable oil - for frying
- 8 ounces goat cheese - room temperature
- 1 lemon – juiced
- 3 tablespoons basil – minced
- 1½ tablespoons chives – minced
- Kosher salt and freshly ground black pepper
- 1 cup all-purpose flour
- 1 cup buttermilk
- 1½ cups yellow cornmeal
- 1 tablespoon garlic powder
- 1 teaspoon paprika
- ¼ teaspoon cayenne
- 4 to 5 green tomatoes

Notes

....

....

....

....

....

....

Truffle Duck Fat Fries

Serves 4 to 6

When Tres and I visited Portland, Maine, we were there approximately thirty-six hours and ate at about fifteen restaurants – no joke. I heard Portland was a culinary dream, so I put together a food tour that included way too many places to eat in one day, but we said, "Ah, let's do it anyway." We walked into each restaurant and shared the best one to two items on every menu. It was so much fun, and I've never been so full. We had truffle duck fat fries at one of the stops, and they stuck with me. This is my re-creation.

- 4 russet potatoes
- 4 to 6 tablespoons duck fat (find it jarred at specialty food stores)
- Truffle or kosher salt and freshly ground black pepper
- 1 tablespoon truffle oil
- 1 teaspoon minced garlic
- 1 teaspoon fresh rosemary - minced
- 1 tablespoon truffle or regular honey
- ½ cup mayonnaise
- Freshly grated Parmesan cheese

Make the fries. Roughly peel the potatoes, leaving some skin on. Cut the potatoes into thick logs - you should get about 16 from each potato. Place in a large bowl, cover in water, and soak for an hour - this will get extra starch out and make them crispy. Drain the potatoes and pat dry with paper towels.

Preheat your oven to 400 degrees. In a large sauté pan, heat 2 tablespoons of duck fat over medium-high heat. In batches, cook the potato logs for about 2 minutes on each side in the duck fat. In between batches, add more duck fat if needed. Line the partially-cooked logs onto a baking sheet covered with foil. Sprinkle lightly with salt and pepper. Roast the potatoes in the oven for about 20 to 25 minutes, or until golden. The last 5 minutes, change the stove setting to broil to get them extra crispy.

Make the mayonnaise dipping sauce. While the potatoes are roasting, heat the truffle oil in a small sauté pan over low heat. Add the garlic and rosemary, and cook for 1 minute, or until fragrant. Transfer to a small bowl and add the honey, mayonnaise, and a pinch of salt. Mix until combined.
🕐 *Refrigerate until ready to use – up to one week.*

When the potatoes come out of the oven, immediately sprinkle them with a little more salt and freshly grated Parmesan cheese. Serve with the prepared mayonnaise sauce.

Notes

....
....
....
....
....
....

Balsamic BBQ Meatballs

As a Southern woman, I can't say I've ever been to a bridal shower, baby shower, party or gathering where meatballs weren't served. They're a staple, and because I love BBQ and Balsamic, I had to create my own version. These are a crowd-pleaser beyond crowd-pleasers.

Make the sauce. In a small saucepan, whisk together the ketchup, balsamic vinegar, brown sugar, Dijon mustard, apple cider vinegar, Worcestershire sauce, garlic powder, and salt over low heat until smooth and warm, about 8 minutes. 🕐 *Sauce can be made ahead and refrigerated for several days.*

Make the meatball mixture. Preheat your oven to 350 degrees. In a large mixing bowl, combine the pork, beef, onion, garlic, Parmesan, cream, beaten egg, basil, salt, and bread crumbs lightly with a fork until it just comes together. (Don't overmix! The lighter the meat is handled, the more tender the meatballs.)

Form the meatballs by using a small ice cream scoop and your hands. Place on a baking sheet lined with parchment paper and spoon a small amount of the Balsamic BBQ sauce over each meatball. Bake for 35 to 40 minutes, or until cooked through. Serve extra sauce alongside for dipping.

Notes

....

....

....

Makes 15 to 20 meatballs

BALSAMIC BBQ SAUCE:
- ⅓ cup ketchup
- ⅓ cup balsamic vinegar
- 2 tablespoons light brown sugar
- 2 tablespoons Dijon mustard
- 1 tablespoon apple cider vinegar
- ½ tablespoon Worcestershire sauce
- ½ teaspoon garlic powder
- ¼ teaspoon kosher salt

MEATBALLS:
- ½ pound ground pork
- ½ pound ground beef
- ⅓ cup grated onion
- 1 garlic clove – minced
- ¼ cup Parmesan cheese
- 1 tablespoon cream or whole milk
- 1 large egg – beaten
- 2 tablespoons minced fresh basil
- 1 teaspoon kosher salt
- 1 cup bread crumbs

Vegetarian & Carnivore Dates

After several years of marriage, it's easy to get into date-night slumps. Life gets busy, work sometimes takes over, and weekends are often filled with things you have to do rather than things you want to do. Tres and I have always made it a point to have fun date nights together throughout the week – it doesn't have to be anything big and a lot of ours happen at home. Of course, we already eat dinner together at home every night, but there are easy ways to make it date-night special. Set the dining room table, use your fancy china, open a bottle of nice wine you have been saving, turn the TV off and play Frank Sinatra in the background and - my personal favorite -put together a three to four course meal so the entire night is spent at the dinner table with multiple bites of food. Either of these date-dishes are a perfect aperitif or first course, getting your "date" night off to a great start.

Goat Cheese Dates:

40 dates

- 1 tablespoon olive oil
- 20 dates – pitted and sliced in half
- Smoked salt
- 8 ounces goat cheese - room temperature
- 2 tablespoons whole milk
- 40 pecan halves - toasted
- Balsamic reduction - for drizzling

Heat a grill pan over high heat and brush with the olive oil. Lightly salt the inside of each date halve with the smoked salt. Grill for one minute on each side, or until dates have dark char marks. Set the dates aside and let cool.

In a small bowl, mix together the milk and goat cheese until smooth. Fill each date halve evenly with the goat cheese mixture. Lightly sprinkle more smoked salt over the goat cheese. Top each with one toasted pecan. Place on a serving platter and drizzle with balsamic reduction.

Bacon Wrapped Date Flight

4 flights, 20 dates

ALL DATES:

- 5 small bowls
- 5 spoons
- 5 pieces of foil - cut approximately 12 inches and folded around the edges to make a wall around each edge
- 10 slices of bacon - cut in half
- 10 dates - pitted and cut in half

MAPLE ESPRESSO DATES:

- 1 tablespoon espresso powder
- 2 tablespoons light brown sugar
- ¼ cup maple syrup

CINNAMON SUGAR DATES:

- 2 tablespoons granulated sugar
- 1 teaspoon ground cinnamon

LEMON ROSEMARY DATES:

- 2 lemons - zested
- 1 teaspoon finely minced rosemary

CHIPOTLE DATES:

- 1 chipotle pepper in adobo sauce
- 2 tablespoons adobo sauce
- 1 teaspoon chili powder
- ½ teaspoon ground cumin

HONEY LAVENDER DATES:

- 3 tablespoons honey
- 1 teaspoon finely minced lavender buds
- ¼ teaspoon vanilla extract

Preheat your oven to 400 degrees. Make the mix for each date flavor. In the first bowl, mix together the espresso, brown sugar, and maple. In the second bowl, mix together the cinnamon and sugar. In the third bowl, mix together the lemon and rosemary. In the fourth bowl, mix together the chipotle pepper, sauce, chili powder, and cumin. In the fifth bowl, mix together the honey, lavender, and vanilla.

Prepare the dates. There should be 20 date halves and 20 bacon halves. Wrap each date, and if necessary, secure with a toothpick. Working with one mix at a time, dip 4 bacon-wrapped dates into each mix, completely covering each date. Place each flavored date on a piece of foil keeping like flavors together. Wash your hands in between dipping dates into each flavor so they don't mix with the others.

Place the foil sheets on two baking sheets - two on one baking sheet, three on the other. It's important that the foil pieces have a wall around each edge so the flavors don't mix – it also makes for easy cleanup. Bake for about 15 minutes, or until bacon is crisp. Plate individually so each person has a "flight." For a casual party, label five small platters with each date flavor or have guests guess the flavors in each.

Salmon Toasts with Truffle Honey

When Tres and I were in Barcelona, we visited the sought-after restaurant, Quimet y Quimet. It's a tiny place that gets completely shoulder-to-shoulder packed the second the doors open. It's all tapas, with only standing room to eat the little bites of food served straight from the bar. When we rolled in, we asked for recommendations, and a guy we met who had been there the day before urged us to get the Truffle Salmon Toast. After taking a bite, we both died right then and there, and of course, it was the first dish I made when I got home the next week.

Preheat your oven to broil. Slice each baguette half into 5 even, square pieces. Drizzle with the olive oil and place under the broiler for 2 to 3 minutes, or until toasted. In a small bowl, mix the ricotta together with one tablespoon of the truffle oil. Evenly spread a thin layer of the ricotta over each slice of toasted bread. Top with the smoked salmon. Drizzle with the honey, balsamic reduction, and the remaining 2 tablespoons of truffle oil.

Notes

Makes 10 toasts

- 1 ciabatta baguette – sliced in half horizontally
- 1 tablespoon olive oil
- 1 cup ricotta cheese
- 3 tablespoons good-quality truffle oil
- 4 ounces thinly sliced smoked salmon – halved
- 3 tablespoons honey
- 1 tablespoon balsamic reduction

BLT Crostini

I have called myself the "BLT Queen" on multiple occasions, as I'm convinced I've made more BLTs than any person ever. Not to mention, I've put just about every ingredient known to man on my different versions. I love a BLT, and I think there are thousands of different ways to make them. This is the perfect party version, and I promise, if you make this your friends and family will think you're a genius in the kitchen.

Make the bacon. Preheat your oven to 325 degrees. In a medium bowl, mix together the brown sugar, chili powder, and paprika. Dip each slice of bacon into the mixture, coating both sides well. Lay flat on a parchment-lined baking sheet. Bake for 15 to 20 minutes, or until crispy. Set aside to cool. Once cool, cut or tear into fourths.

Make the aioli. Place the garlic, egg yolks, lemon juice, mustard, and salt in the bowl of a food processor. Blend together until well combined. With the processor still running, slowly pour in the olive oil in a thin, steady stream. It should be a pale-yellow color when finished. Add the basil and pulse a few times. 🕐 *Refrigerate until ready to use – up to one week.*

Make the BLTs. Slice each tomato into 8 slices. Sprinkle with salt and pepper. Build the crostini.

Spoon a thin layer of aioli on each crostini. Top with arugula, a slice of the tomato, and a piece of the bacon. Finish with a drizzle of olive oil and white balsamic reduction.

Makes 32 crostini

CANDIED BACON:
- ⅓ cup light brown sugar
- 2 teaspoons chili powder
- 1 teaspoon smoked paprika
- 8 slices bacon

AIOLI:
- 1 large garlic clove - chopped
- 2 egg yolks
- ½ lemon - juiced
- ½ teaspoon Dijon mustard
- Kosher salt
- ⅓ cup good-quality extra virgin olive oil
- ¼ cup chopped basil

BLT:
- 4 Roma tomatoes
- 32 toasted crostini
- 2 cups arugula – roughly chopped
- Good-quality extra virgin olive oil – for drizzling
- White balsamic reduction – for drizzling

Notes

Smoked Oyster Bites

Makes 20
to 25 bites

Tres's dad, Frank is one of the best home cooks I've ever met, but back in my picky days there were certain foods he cooked that I was scared to try. The good news is, all those things I "thought" I didn't like became some of my favorite foods – escargot, caviar, oysters and even these smoked oyster bites with – wait for it – CANNED smoked oysters. Gasp! If you've never had canned smoked oysters, I know what you're thinking because at one time I thought the same thing. They're actually really, really delightful though. The first time I had these crackers, I couldn't stop eating them. Now, I always have a can of smoked oysters in my pantry to whip up this simple, yet elegant and beautifully presented appetizer.

- 1 (8-ounce) package cream cheese - room temperature
- 20 to 25 fancy, round crackers
- 1 (3-ounce) can smoked oysters - drained and rinsed
- Hot pepper jelly
- 20 to 25 sprigs fresh dill
- Fleur de sel (or flaky sea salt)

Spread a generous amount of the cream cheese on each cracker and top with a single smoked oyster. If you don't have enough oysters for each cracker, cut larger ones in half to make extra. Spoon a dollop of hot pepper jelly over each oyster. Top each with a sprig of dill and sprinkle of fleur de sel. Serve on a white platter for beautiful presentation

Notes

Fleur de sel is a high-quality French finishing salt that can be found in specialty grocery stores. It can be pricy, but a little goes a long way – I keep the same container for a year or more. If you can't get fleur de sel, substitute with flaky sea salt.

Supersonic Gin and Tonic

Serves 1,
plus simple syrup

Growing up in the 90s, it was nearly impossible not to fall in love with the rock music of that era. To this very day, 90s rock is still my favorite music. I'll be honest; I rarely listen to anything aside from 80s hairband and 90s grunge and alternative – I live by it. When we were tweens, my brother and I would sit in his room listening to just about every rock CD that came out that year on repeat, so the music is very nostalgic for me. Oasis was always one of my favorite bands, and if you're a fan, you'll know where I got the name for this cocktail. If not, I think you should look them up and take a listen! "I'm feeling Supersonic, Give me gin and tonic. You can have it all but how much do you want it?"

M ake the rosemary anise simple syrup. In a saucepan, bring the sugar, water, rosemary, and star anise to a boil. Set aside to steep and cool. Strain and transfer to a bottle or container and refrigerate until ready to use.

Make the cocktail. Halfway fill a gin balloon glass or extra-large wine glass with ice cubes. Add the gin, simple syrup, and orange juice. Stir together with a bar spoon or regular spoon, and as stirring, slowly pour in the tonic water. Add the fresh orange slice, rosemary, and star anise to the glass and stir once more.

ROSEMARY ANISE
SIMPLE SYRUP:
- ½ cup sugar
- ½ cup water
- 4 sprigs fresh rosemary
- 3 whole star anise

COCKTAIL:
- Ice cubes
- 2 ounces gin
- 1 ounce rosemary anise simple syrup
- 1 tablespoon fresh squeezed orange juice
- ½ to ¾ cup tonic water
- 1 fresh orange slice
- 1 sprig fresh rosemary
- 2 to 3 whole star anise

Notes

French Inspired Sangria

Wine trips are Tres's and my favorite holidays. We have visited numerous wine regions, but one of the most memorable wines trips was our drive from Paris to Epernay and Reims, the Champagne region of France. The first day we popped into a small shop in the village, and a little visit turned into a head-start on drinking and learning about Champagne. The shop owner and his friend were sitting behind the counter talking, laughing and sampling multiple bottles of Champagne and asked us to join them. They barely spoke English and we barely spoke French, but somehow we chatted with them for several hours, going through several bottles of the good stuff. We were even introduced to one of their friends, a winemaker and owner of one of the bottles we were drinking. It was such a glorious experience, we lost track of time and almost missed our Moët & Chandon appointment. That was one of the most authentic, local experiences we've ever had in another country. This cocktail is inspired by that trip and our hope is to experience many more holidays just like that one.

M ake the honey-lavender-berry simple syrup. In a saucepan, bring the honey, water, lavender, and ¼ cup each of the strawberries, cherries, and raspberries to a boil. Slightly mash the berries in the syrup and set aside to cool.

Assemble the sangria. Add the remaining berries to a pitcher. Slice a lemon in half and juice one half into the pitcher. Slice the other half into small pieces and add with the berries. Strain the syrup into the pitcher, discarding the mashed berries and lavender. Add the Lillet® and the bottle of sparkling rose into the pitcher. Stir together and serve.

Makes 1 pitcher

- ½ cup honey
- 1 cup water
- 2 lavender sprigs
- ¾ cup of strawberries – sliced
- ¾ cup of Rainier cherries - pitted and halved
- ¾ cup red raspberries
- 1 lemon
- 1 cup rose Lillet® – chilled
- 1 bottle sparkling rose champagne – chilled

Notes

....
....
....
....
....

Fireside Pisco

Serves 1,
plus simple syrup

As I get older, I appreciate a good, cold winter more and more. Sitting by the fire with a cup of something cozy to warm my bones makes me happier than any hot summer day ever could. A glass of bold cabernet or better yet, a good-quality, buttery chardonnay are hard to beat when bundled up fireside, but sometimes a wintery cocktail is just necessary. This one is inspired by three of my all time favorite drinks: coffee, apple cider and a pisco sour.

Make the apple cider simple syrup. In a saucepan, bring the sugar, apple juice, water, and apple pie spice to a boil. Set aside to steep and cool. Transfer to a bottle or container and refrigerate until ready to use.

Make the cocktail. Fill a cocktail shaker with ice. Add the Baileys, Pisco, Frangelico, simple syrup, and heavy cream if using. Shake several times and strain into a lowball or whisky glass.

Notes

APPLE CIDER
SIMPLE SYRUP:

- ½ cup granulated sugar
- ½ cup apple juice
- ½ cup water
- ½ teaspoon apple pie spice

COCKTAIL:

- Ice
- 2 ounces Baileys Irish Creme
- 1 ounce Pisco
- ½ ounce Frangelico
- ½ ounce apple cider simple syrup
- Dash heavy cream, optional

Simple syrups can be refrigerated for up to 6 months.

Lady Squirrel

The Pink Lady, a gin-based cocktail, was created during Prohibition. It was also one of the first recipes I made after my grandmother passed down our historical family cookbook to me. Maybe my intense love for all things 1920s played into it (seriously, I'm addicted to reading Hemingway and Fitzgerald biographies) or maybe it was the cute name – either way, it became one of my favorite cocktails. When I discovered there was a similar version called a Pink Squirrel, but with a slight almond, chocolate flavor, I decided these two drinks needed to become one, so I created the Lady Squirrel. Using the exact Pink Lady recipe from my family cookbook and a traditional Pink Squirrel recipe, the Lady Squirrel is divine and dainty.

Fill a shaker with ice. Add the gin, Crème de Cacao, Crème de Noyaux, half-and-half, and egg white. Shake vigorously for about 30 seconds. Strain into a vintage stemmed cocktail glass.

Notes

....

....

....

Serves 1

- Ice
- 1 ounce gin
- 1 ounce Crème de Cacao
- 1 ounce Crème de Noyaux
- 1 ounce half-and-half
- 1 egg white

For those of you scared of drinking an egg white, vigorous shaking (or whipping in a blender – like in the Seersucker Punch) practically cooks it. An egg white is put in many bar-served cocktails to make them creamy and frothy. You've more than likely drank an egg white before if you wonder how that cocktail from the bar was so fluffy, bubbly, creamy, and delicious. Bonus - high-protein, less calories and fat.

Seersucker Punch

Serves 12 to 15

When spring rolls around, every Southerner on earth can't wait to break out the seersucker – dresses, pants, shoes, shirts – you name it and we got it in seersucker. When it comes to this fun fabric, I can't help but think of the FedEx St. Jude Classic golf tournament. It's a huge event for Memphians and a big excuse to wear seersucker on Seersucker Sunday of the tournament, one of our favorite days to attend. My pretty galfriends in their seersucker dresses at bridal showers and spring parties also comes to mind, which is why I decided we needed a fun drink to go with all the lovely ensembles. Punch is the perfect spring party drink and this one is creamy, sweet, delicious and spiked.

- ½ cup granulated sugar
- ½ cup water
- 1 tablespoon vanilla paste
- 1 ½ cups vanilla vodka
- 1 ½ cups blue curaçao
- 3 cups ice
- 1 ½ cups egg whites
- ¾ cup heavy cream
- 2 cups sparkling water

Make the vanilla simple syrup. In a saucepan, bring the sugar, water, and vanilla paste to a boil. Set aside to steep and cool.

Make the punch. Pour the vodka, blue curaçao, ice, egg whites, heavy cream, sparkling water, and cooled vanilla syrup into a high-speed blender. Blend together until ice is completely incorporated and egg whites are whipped. Pour into a small punch bowl and serve.

Notes

....

....

....

Vanilla paste is a rich, concentrated syrup made with vanilla beans. I use it when I want the vanilla flavor in something to really stand out. It can be substituted with vanilla bean seeds or vanilla extract.

Holiday Simple Syrup

Approximately
3 cups

Because I spend so much time in my kitchen throughout the holiday season, I'm the worst when it comes to last-minute shopping for gifts. I decided years ago to just make it easy on myself – make gifts in the kitchen! My friends and family are thrilled when they open up these little bottles of joy. They're also the perfect hostess gift for holiday parties. This simple syrup can be used numerous ways – in cocktails, mocktails, coffee and even over ice cream or cake! Two of my go-to holiday recipes include a tablespoon of this syrup in a champagne flute, topped with Champagne or sparkling water.

- 2 cups granulated sugar
- 2 cups water
- 1 (3-inch piece) fresh ginger – peeled and sliced
- ¼ cup cinnamon candies
- 2 cinnamon sticks
- 2 whole star anise
- 10 cloves
- 1 teaspoon vanilla extract
- ⅛ teaspoon freshly grated nutmeg

Stir the sugar, water, ginger, cinnamon candies, cinnamon sticks, anise, cloves, vanilla extract, and nutmeg together in a medium saucepan. Place the pan over high heat, and let come to a boil for one minute. Set aside to steep and cool. Using a small, plastic funnel, transfer the syrup to decorative bottles, label, and tie with a ribbon or your choice of holiday cheer.

Simple syrups can be stored in your refrigerator for up to 6 months.

Notes

....

....

....

Reminisce & Relish
Your Keepsake Recipes

Short Stories

SALADS & SOUPS

"Oh, a little won't hurt."

My entire life Mama always said, "A little bit of anything never hurt anyone." Mostly regarding food, but as I grew up, I realized it also had a lot to do with life. I didn't have a strict upbringing by any means - quite the opposite, actually. My brother and I joke now that we had a hippie mom. Though very conservative in most of her thinking, her parenting was loose as a goose. So long as we weren't acting like brats, being disrespectful or breaking obvious rules, she let us be free as birds. Mama believed too many rules and strict parenting backfired into rebellion, and she must have been right because my brother and I were both well-behaved kids who made good decisions. All the kids I knew in school who were always into trouble or partying seemed to be told no a lot by their parents. Mama would say, "Why say no when you can say yes?"

Food was a huge part of that equation. Mama never forced us to eat all the food on our plates at dinner, and she truly let us be kids when it came to what we ate. My My Nenne, my Mama's mother also had a few opinions about food. When someone refused a piece of cake or avoided something fried, I remember hearing her say, "Oh, a little won't hurt." I guess like grandmother, like mother, like daughter because anytime someone turns their nose up at something a little unhealthy, I've caught myself many times saying, "Just eat it. A little won't hurt you." Three generations strong and while I do believe that a little won't hurt, I'm all about balance. As humans we must eat healthy on most occasions to get the nutrition our bodies need. This chapter is all about that balance. These salads and soups are full of greens, protein and healthful ingredients. But because a little won't hurt, there are a few splurges along the way.

Super Southern Salad

Serves 4

I grew up in Mississippi right outside of Memphis, Tennessee, so Southern food was always the focal point of any celebration. The Down-South ingredients in this salad remind me a lot of my childhood. Most kids love anything fried and sweet. The fried grits and sweet dressing in this dish will have you welcoming this salad with open arms. I bet this is one bowl of greens you can even get your kids to eat.

- 3 tablespoons balsamic vinegar
- 2 tablespoons maple syrup
- 2 teaspoons lemon juice
- 1 teaspoon Dijonnaise
- Kosher salt and freshly ground black pepper
- ¼ cup good-quality extra virgin olive oil
- 1 cup vegetable oil
- ¾ cup cooked stone-ground grits - chilled
- ½ cup all-purpose flour
- 2 large eggs – beaten
- 1 cup panko bread crumbs
- 1 Fuji apple – sliced thin
- 8 cups mixed greens
- ½ cup praline or candied pecans – roughly chopped
- ¼ cup dried cranberries

Make the dressing. Combine the balsamic vinegar, maple syrup, lemon juice, Dijonnaise, a dash of salt and pepper, and olive oil by whisking in a small bowl or shaking in a Mason jar.

Make the grit croutons. In a medium saucepan, heat the vegetable oil to 350 degrees. Make 1 tablespoon balls with the grits by rolling each in your hand until round. Place the flour, beaten eggs, and panko bread crumbs in 3 separate bowls. Dredge the balls in the flour, dip in the egg mixture, and then cover in the panko. Fry for 2 to 3 minutes, or until golden. Using a slotted spoon, transfer to a paper towel-lined plate to drain and sprinkle with salt when they come out of the oil.

When ready to serve, toss the apples and greens with the dressing in a salad bowl. Sprinkle with the pecans, cranberries, and top with the grit croutons.

Notes

....

....

....

Spiced Citrus Salad

Serves 4

Citrus tastes like spring and summer to me - so the peak season falling in the middle of winter has always thrown me off a bit. I decided a few years ago that the reason for this is to get our taste buds ready for spring. Because of the beautiful pink color of fresh grapefruit and deep red hue of blood orange, I decided to try this salad on Valentine's Day. The flavors are clean and bright – the perfect foretaste of warmer seasons – with the coriander and pepper flake dressing keeping it a little warm, snuggly, and wintery.

- 1 lemon – juiced
- 1 tablespoon white balsamic reduction
- 2 teaspoons agave nectar
- 1 teaspoon ground coriander
- ¼ teaspoon red pepper flakes
- Kosher salt and freshly ground black pepper
- ¼ cup good-quality extra virgin olive oil
- 1 grapefruit
- 2 oranges
- 2 blood oranges or tangerines
- 4 cups spinach and arugula mix - roughly chopped
- ½ red onion - sliced thin (optional)

Make the dressing. Combine the lemon juice, white balsamic reduction, agave, coriander, red pepper flakes, a dash of salt and pepper, and the olive oil by whisking in a small bowl or shaking in a Mason jar.

Make the salad. Slice the grapefruit, oranges, and blood oranges into ¼-inch rounds. For each round, cut the peel off, removing the skin. Lightly sprinkle the slices with salt and pepper.

In a large bowl, place the spinach and arugula mix and toss together with ¾ of the salad dressing. Spread the spinach and arugula mix on a large platter. Top with the citrus rounds, layering the different colors. Add the sliced red onion, if using, and drizzle the remaining dressing over the top.

Notes

Peach Burrata Salad

Serves 4

As a self-taught chef, there's nothing more rewarding than writing your first recipe, cooking it, tasting it and realizing you nailed it. Because fresh peaches were the first ingredient I ever created a dish around, I'll never look at them the same again. This is not the first recipe I wrote but it is one of the best peach recipes I've ever eaten. The combination of sweet peaches, creamy burrata and peppery arugula make this salad summer on a plate.

In a medium bowl, toss the arugula and mint together. Combine the white balsamic reduction, lemon juice, a dash of salt and pepper, and the olive oil by whisking in a small bowl or shaking in a Mason jar. Pour the dressing on the greens and toss together. Evenly distribute the salad mixture onto four small plates. Lightly sprinkle the peaches with salt and place on top of each salad.

In a small bowl, toss the almonds, honey, and cinnamon together until coated. Sprinkle about 2 tablespoons of almonds on each salad then top with 2 ounces of sliced burrata. Salt and pepper the burrata and drizzle white balsamic reduction over the top.

- 4 cups arugula
- 2 cups mint leaves - roughly chopped
- 1 tablespoon white balsamic reduction, plus more for drizzling
- 3 tablespoons fresh lemon juice
- Kosher salt and freshly ground black pepper
- ¼ cup good-quality extra virgin olive oil
- 2 peaches – pitted and sliced
- ½ cup sliced almonds - toasted
- 2 teaspoons honey
- 1 teaspoon ground cinnamon
- 8 ounces burrata cheese - sliced

Notes

....

....

....

📌 *Balsamic reduction can be found in grocery stores or made by cooking balsamic vinegar in a saucepan over medium-low heat for about 15 to 20 minutes or until reduced and syrupy.*

Very Merry Salad

When I was in elementary school, I read a book every year around the holidays about a family in the Victorian era celebrating Christmas. The chapter about their Christmas dinner seemed like a dream to me. They were dressed up, fancy china and silverware lined the table, a gorgeous turkey was the centerpiece with bountiful sides to accompany – it's just how I wanted Christmas dinner to be when I grew up and could host my own. Now, every Christmas at my home, this is the scene I try to replicate. This salad is so beautiful it could easily be a holiday table centerpiece, plus it's healthy and delicious.

- ¼ cup good-quality extra virgin olive oil
- 3 tablespoons apple cider vinegar
- 1 ½ tablespoons maple syrup
- 1 teaspoon pumpkin pie spice
- 1 teaspoon Dijon mustard
- ½ teaspoon kosher salt
- 2 bunches kale - rinsed, dried, stems removed, and chopped
- 1 cup walnuts – toasted
- 1 pomegranate – seeded
- ½ cup dried cranberries or cherries

Make the dressing. Combine the olive oil, apple cider vinegar, maple syrup, pumpkin pie spice, Dijon, and salt by whisking in a small bowl or shaking in a mason jar.

Make the salad. In a salad bowl, toss the chopped kale with the dressing until all the greens are covered. Sprinkle the walnuts, pomegranate seeds, and dried cranberries over the top.

🕐 *Serve immediately or refrigerate for up to one day.*

Notes

....

....

....

Provence Salad

Serves 4

Years ago I read the oldest living person ever lived to be 122 years old and hailed from the south of France – the Provence region to be exact. She claimed she rode her bike until she was one-hundred, put olive oil on everything she ate, consumed two pounds of chocolate a week and drank Port wine every day – sounds like a pretty gleeful life to me! The point is, after my visit to Provence – seeing the way people live and what they eat – I believe in some way that may have contributed to her extended life. In the French countryside and even larger cities in the Provence region people are active – biking everywhere they go. Their food consumption is healthful, fresh and clean – sure, they love butter, bread and rich foods as much as we do in the South, but they eat it in moderation. And there's a farmer's market full of homegrown, wholesome produce, meat and cheese on every corner. Seeing the way people live there is inspiring. It makes you want to never eat processed food again, get rid of your car and bike to a farmer's market every day for your meals. This salad is all the things I love about Provence – lavender, fresh olive oil, honey, French bread and the simplicity of clean, healthy eating.

- ½ loaf French bread – cut into ½-inch cubes
- 3 tablespoons olive oil
- 2 tablespoons Herbes de Provence
- 1 teaspoons kosher salt, plus a dash
- 3 tablespoons freshly squeezed lemon juice
- 2 teaspoons lavender (or regular) honey
- 1 teaspoon Dijon mustard
- Freshly ground black pepper
- ¼ cup good-quality extra virgin olive oil
- 2 bunches green leaf lettuce – rinsed, dried, and chopped
- ½ cup shaved Parmesan cheese

Notes

....
....
....
....
....
....

Preheat your oven to 375 degrees. On a large baking sheet, toss the bread cubes together with the olive oil, Herbes de Provence, and 1 teaspoon of salt, until evenly coated. Bake for 10 to 15 minutes or until golden and crispy.

Combine the lemon juice, honey, Dijon, a dash of salt and pepper, and the olive oil by whisking in a small bowl or shaking in a Mason jar. In a large salad bowl, toss the lettuce, half the croutons, and half the Parmesan with the salad dressing. Top with the remaining croutons and Parmesan.

Herbes de Provence can be found on the spice aisle in the grocery store.

Fig Salad with Marinated Mozzarella

Sometimes old friends are the best friends. I absolutely loved high school. I made some great friends there and have memories that still make me fall on the floor laughing. I don't get to see my high school girlfriends very often (funny enough, the one I see the most, Tina, lives in Vegas), but when we all get together, it's like we didn't miss a beat in time. Last year, I met my best high school friends, Stephanie, Erin and Cassie, for the first time in years. It was the most fun I'd had in a long time (and anyone who knows me knows - I'm always having fun). The night consisted of reminiscing, catching up and actual tears from laughing so hard. We swore we would get together more often, but even though it didn't seem like that long, it took us another year to get together again. Factual proof that the older you get, the busier life gets and the quicker time passes. This salad makes me think of "ladies who lunch," and I think it's the perfect excuse to get a group of old galfriends together you never get to see. It's light, feminine and sweet as pie – just like your girlfriends. Even if it's been ages, be the first one to reach out to old friends. They probably miss seeing you too. And I promise, you will pick up right where you left off.

Prep the bocconcini. Put the bocconcini in a bowl. Add the olive oil, lemon zest and juice, and herbs.

🕐 *Toss together and refrigerate for at least one hour or for several days.*

Make the candied Marcona almonds. Heat your oven to 350 degrees. Place the almonds, sugar, cardamom, salt, and water in a small saucepan. Bring to a boil for 3 minutes, take off the heat, and transfer to a baking sheet lined with parchment paper. Bake for about 5 to 7 minutes, or until the nuts are golden. Let cool and then break into pieces.

Build the salad. Toss the mixed greens and arugula together in a salad bowl or large serving platter. Evenly place the figs, marinated bocconcini, and candied Marcona almonds over the greens. Lightly squeeze lemon juice over the salad, drizzle olive oil over the top, and sprinkle with Fleur de Sel or kosher salt.

Serves 4

MOZZARELLA:
- 8 ounces bocconcini (mini mozzarella balls) – liquid drained
- 4 tablespoons olive oil
- 1 lemon – zested and juiced
- ¼ cup finely minced fresh mint and basil

CANDIED MARCONA ALMONDS:
- ⅓ cup whole Marcona almonds
- ¼ cup granulated sugar
- 2 teaspoons ground cardamom
- ½ teaspoon kosher salt
- 3 tablespoons water

SALAD:
- 2 cups mixed greens
- 2 cups arugula
- 10 to 15 fresh figs – sliced
- Lemon juice
- Extra virgin olive oil
- Fleur de Sel or kosher salt

Notes

Mexican Restaurant "Sick Day" Soup

Serves 4 to 6

My parents and I have a tradition – any time we meet for lunch, we go to a Mexican restaurant. We love Mexican food but we particularly love sopa de pollo. It's a dish my Pop started ordering years ago. Mama and I caught on and ever since our order looks like this: one large cheese dip and three sopa de pollos. It's also become a go-to staple for us when we're sick. The soup has light, yet comforting elements to it, making it a perfect replacement for typical chicken noodle. It also has a slight spice that makes it the ideal medicine for a stuffy nose. I re-created it so I don't have to speed-dial a restaurant when I'm sick, and it can be frozen so it's on-hand for any sick day. It's also a great detox, health soup. It's my first choice for dinner to get my body back on track after traveling or a long weekend of unhealthy eating.

In a large Dutch oven or pot, heat the olive oil over medium-high heat. Salt and pepper the chicken breasts liberally on both sides. Lightly brown the chicken in the oil on all sides, about 5 minutes. Set aside on a plate. Roughly chop one of the onions and finely chop the other. Set aside the finely chopped onion. Add the roughly chopped onion, garlic cloves, bell pepper, and jalapeño to the pot with a dash of salt and pepper. Sauté for about 5 minutes, or until onions and peppers are soft. Add the chili powder, cumin, dried oregano, and bay leaves. Stir together and let cook for another 2 minutes. Stir in the tomato paste, celery, carrots, cilantro, chicken stock, and browned chicken breasts. Bring to a boil for about 2 minutes and then lower the heat and simmer for 1 hour.

Take the chicken out and let cool. Strain all the veggies out of the pot and discard until left with just broth. Once the chicken is cool enough to handle, shred into pieces, discarding the skin and bones. Add the shredded chicken, diced tomatoes with green chilies, and finely chopped onion to the pot with the broth and cook over low for 10 more minutes. Add the chopped cilantro and about 2 teaspoons of salt, plus more to taste. If using, add the cooked rice. Serve with avocado and lime if desired.

- 1 tablespoon olive oil
- Kosher salt and freshly ground black pepper
- 2 chicken breasts – bone in, skin on
- 2 white onions
- 3 garlic cloves – peeled and smashed
- 1 green bell pepper – seeded and chopped
- 2 small jalapeño peppers – seeded and chopped
- 1 tablespoon chili powder
- ½ tablespoon ground cumin
- 1 teaspoon dried oregano
- 2 bay leaves
- 2 tablespoons tomato paste
- 3 celery sticks – roughly chopped
- 3 carrots – peeled and roughly chopped
- 1 handful (about 1 cup) fresh cilantro, plus ½ cup - chopped
- 12 cups low-sodium chicken stock
- 4 (10-ounce) cans diced tomatoes with green chilies – drained
- 2 cups cooked white rice (optional)
- Avocado – sliced (optional)
- Limes – quartered (optional)

Serve immediately, refrigerate for up to 3 days, or store in plastic containers in the freezer – up to 3 months – for a sick day or a cook-free night.

Traditional Halloween Chili

I look forward to October 31st all year. For me Halloween isn't just a holiday – it's a season! The first day of October, the celebration begins at our house. I decorate the house the first week, watch scary movies every day and plan everything from hayrides and pumpkin patches to haunted houses and Hallows' Eve get-togethers. The weekend before the big day, Tres and I throw a huge "Monster Bash" for a big group of friends. We like to keep the day of Halloween reserved for trick-or-treaters and a small group of friends who come over for chili and scary movies. This recipe is the original Halloween Chili and has been my go-to every scary movie night. Mama has one of the best chili recipes ever, so I took her recipe for inspiration and created this one. Don't let the long list of ingredients intimidate you – it's a quick and easy one-pot recipe with tons of flavor.

In an extra-large soup pot over medium-high heat, cook and drain the ground beef, ground bison, and chorizo each one at a time. Set all the cooked meats aside on a large plate. Wipe the pot out and fry the bacon. Set the bacon aside with the meat, leaving the grease in the pot. Heat the bacon grease and butter over medium heat. Add the onion with a dash of salt and pepper and sauté for about 8 minutes, or until they start to soften. Add the poblano peppers, green bell pepper, red bell pepper, and jalapeño pepper with another dash of salt, and sauté until soft. Add the garlic and cook one more minute, stirring everything together well.

Transfer all the meat back into the pot with the veggies. Add the brown sugar, chili powder, oregano, garlic powder, cumin, smoked paprika, cayenne, and about 1 tablespoon of salt. Stir the spices together with the meat and veggies and let cook for about 3 to 4 minutes.

Add the chopped chipotles and adobo sauce, San Marzano tomatoes (continuing to break the whole tomatoes up into pieces), tomato paste, chili sauce, kidney beans, chili beans, and chicken stock. Stir together and let come to a slight bubble. Lower the heat and let simmer. Taste and add more salt if needed.

🕑 *Serve immediately, refrigerate for up to 3 days, or freeze in plastic containers for up to 3 months.*

Notes

....

....

....

📌 *Serve with cooked pasta, tortilla chips, sour cream, shredded cheese, avocado, chopped onions, or whatever your heart desires.*

Serves 8 to 10

- 1 pound ground beef
- 1 pound ground bison
- 1 pound ground chorizo
- 4 slices of bacon - diced
- 2 tablespoons unsalted butter
- 2 onions – chopped
- Kosher salt and freshly ground black pepper
- 3 poblano peppers - seeded and chopped
- 1 green bell pepper - seeded and chopped
- 1 red bell pepper - seeded and chopped
- 1 jalapeño pepper - seeded and chopped
- 6 garlic cloves - minced
- ¼ cup light brown sugar
- 4 tablespoons chili powder
- 1 tablespoon dried oregano
- 1 tablespoon garlic powder
- 1 tablespoon ground cumin
- 2 teaspoons smoked paprika
- ½ teaspoon cayenne
- 2 chipotle peppers in adobo sauce - minced, plus two tablespoons of the sauce
- 2 (32-ounce) cans whole San Marzano tomatoes - broken up
- ⅓ cup tomato paste
- ¾ cup chili sauce
- 2 (15-ounce) cans kidney beans
- 2 (15-ounce) cans mild chili beans
- 2 cups low-sodium chicken stock, plus more to thin the chili

Pumpkin Short Rib Halloween Chili

My abnormal obsession with Halloween is completely nostalgic as it goes back to my best childhood memories. For my family, fall wasn't about football and pumpkin spice lattes – it was about Halloween. My dad made it magical, going to extremes with decorations and having my brother and I help. We'd make scarecrows from old flannel shirts, line the driveway with pumpkins and hay bales and put monsters in trees. He bought a new scary mask every year and would play tricks on everyone. I treasure those days and remember telling Mama, "Fall is special. I can smell it when it comes." That stands true today. To add to that crisp, clean fall smell, I keep a pot of chili on the stove - or in the slow cooker - all month. This one can be prepped the night before and plugged in the next day. The short ribs are fall-apart tender and the pumpkin and spices add warmth - a rich, cozy fall combination. This recipe has become a friend favorite and is requested every October, giving it the subtitle, Halloween Chili II.

In a large pot, bring 5 cups water to a boil. Add the short ribs and let boil for 2 minutes. Lower the heat and simmer for 10 minutes. Remove from the heat and let sit for 10 minutes. Drain the ribs and pat dry to remove some of the fat.

In another large pot or Dutch oven, heat 1 tablespoon of the olive oil over medium-high heat. Salt, pepper, and sear all sides of the short ribs until brown. Set the ribs aside on a plate. In the same pot, add the other tablespoon of olive oil, onions, garlic, bell pepper, and a heavy pinch of salt. Cook until soft. Add the chipotle peppers with sauce, chili powder, cumin, oregano, and brown sugar. Stir together and let cook for 2 minutes.

Dump the cooked veggies into a slow-cooker. Add the maple syrup, tomatoes, beef broth, pumpkin purée, and black beans. Stir to combine. Nestle the short ribs into the liquid. Sprinkle the cloves in at the very top so you can find them to discard later.

🕐 *Cover and refrigerate if prepping for the following night.*

When ready to cook, heat the slow-cooker on low. Cook for 6 to 8 hours, or until short ribs are fall-apart tender. Uncover the cooked chili and discard the cloves. Transfer the short ribs to a plate or cutting board. Remove and discard the bones and fat. Shred the short rib meat into small pieces with two forks or your hands. Skim the surface of the chili to remove any extra fat. Add the shredded meat back into the slow cooker, and stir in the cinnamon. Taste the chili, and add more salt if needed.

🕐 *Serve immediately, refrigerate for up to 3 days, or freeze in plastic containers for up to 3 months.*

Serve with green onions and sour cream if desired.

Notes

....

....

....

Serves 6 to 8

- 2 ½ pounds short ribs
- Kosher salt and freshly ground black pepper
- 2 tablespoons olive oil
- 1 large onion – chopped
- 2 garlic cloves – minced
- 1 orange bell pepper – chopped
- 3 chipotle peppers in adobo sauce – chopped, plus 1 tablespoon of the sauce
- 2 tablespoons chili powder
- 1 tablespoon ground cumin
- 1 teaspoon dried oregano
- 2 tablespoons light brown sugar
- ¼ cup maple syrup
- 2 (10-ounce) cans diced tomatoes with green chilies
- 4 cups low-sodium beef broth
- 1 (15-ounce) can pumpkin purée
- 2 (15-ounce) cans black beans – drained and rinsed
- 4 whole cloves
- 2 teaspoons ground cinnamon
- Chopped green onions (optional)
- Sour cream (optional)

Chicken Chowder

Several years ago Tres and I decided with our friends, Kara and Corey, to start traveling over the week of Thanksgiving. It's a great travel time for us because Tres is off work the entire week and there's not the typical Christmas week craziness to worry about. Last year, instead of the four of us going overseas, we decided to pay a visit to Kara and Corey at their new home in Salt Lake City. We spent some of the week at a fabulous resort in Park City and Thanksgiving Day cooking at their house. Because it was a winter wonderland while we were there and my love for snow, it was an amazing Thanksgiving for me. I was inspired to write this recipe while we were there, so I call it the ultimate snow day recipe. However, when fresh corn is in season, it's also the perfect summer soup. You decide.

Heat a large Dutch oven or pot over medium heat. Fry the bacon until crisp. Add the onion and celery and season with salt and pepper. Let cook until the vegetables are soft and translucent. Add the garlic and chipotle peppers, and cook for one more minute. Melt the butter over the top then sprinkle in the flour. Stir together, creating a roux, for 3 to 4 minutes. Pour in the apple brandy, scraping up the brown bits from the bottom of the pan, and let the liquid reduce by half. Increase the heat to high, then add the chicken stock, corn, and shredded chicken. Let the mixture come to a slight boil and then lower the heat to a simmer for a few minutes. Stir in the half-and-half and parsley. Taste for seasoning, adding more salt and pepper if needed.

🕐 *Soup can be refrigerated for several days or frozen in plastic containers for up to 3 months.*

Serves 6 to 8

- 4 slices bacon – cut into strips
- 1 large onion – diced
- 3 sticks celery – diced
- Kosher salt and freshly ground black pepper
- 4 garlic cloves - minced
- 3 chipotle peppers in adobo sauce – minced
- 2 tablespoons unsalted butter
- ½ cup all-purpose flour
- ¼ cup apple brandy
- 6 cups chicken stock
- 2 ears corn – shucked, kernels shaved off the cob
- 1 whole smoked (or rotisserie) chicken – skin removed, meat shredded
- ¼ - ½ cup half-and-half
- 2 tablespoons minced parsley

Notes

....

....

....

....

....

....

Butternut Squash Soup with Apple Relish

I think everyone has a favorite season to cook. No doubt, each season's fresh produce and flavor profiles are special, but I decided a long time ago there must be a season that gets every cook a little more excited to gather family and friends at their table. Like I discussed in my chili story, I have a certain longing for fall. When it comes to cooking, the flavors of autumn seem to make more sense to me than any others. Fall flavors are meant for soups - and apples and squash make this the ultimate fall soup.

Roast the veggies. Preheat your oven to 425 degrees. On a large baking sheet, toss the squash, potatoes, and carrots with 2 tablespoons of olive oil and a heavy sprinkle of salt and pepper. Roast the veggies for 35 minutes or until soft.

Make the soup. While the veggies are roasting, in a Dutch oven or large pot, heat 1 tablespoon of olive oil over medium heat. Sauté the onion and celery with a dash of salt until translucent. Add the garlic to the pot and cook for another minute. Add the vinegar or brandy, chicken stock, maple syrup, sage, cinnamon, nutmeg, cayenne, and roasted veggies and stir to combine. Using a hand blender (or an electric blender working in batches), blend the soup until smooth. Let the soup sit over low heat for 30 minutes or more - the longer it sits, the better it tastes.

Make the relish. In a medium bowl, stir together the apple, walnuts, red onion, cranberries, maple syrup, and a dash salt.

To serve. Make the squash bowls by cutting the pointy corner off the bottom, creating a flat surface for it to sit on. Then cut about 1 inch off the top. Using a spoon, scoop out the seeds and insides until smooth and in the shape of a bowl. Taste the soup before serving and add more salt if needed. Ladle the soup into the squash bowls - or regular bowls - and top with apple relish.

🕐 *Soup can be refrigerated for several days or frozen in plastic containers for up to 3 months.*

Notes

_____

_____

_____

SOUP:

- 2 large butternut squash – peeled, seeded, and chopped into 1-inch pieces
- 1 sweet potato - peeled and chopped into 1-inch pieces
- 1 carrot - peeled and chopped into 1-inch pieces
- 3 tablespoons olive oil
- Kosher salt and freshly ground black pepper
- 1 small onion – chopped
- 1 stalk of celery – chopped
- 2 tablespoons garlic – chopped
- 2 tablespoons apple cider vinegar or apple brandy
- 6 cups low-sodium chicken stock, plus more to thin the soup as desired

2 tablespoons maple syrup

- 1 tablespoon fresh sage – minced
- 1 teaspoon ground cinnamon
- ¼ teaspoon freshly grated nutmeg
- ⅛ teaspoon cayenne

RELISH:

- 1 Fuji Apple – diced small
- ¼ cup walnuts - toasted and finely chopped
- ¼ cup red onion - finely chopped
- ¼ cup dried cranberries - finely chopped
- 2 tablespoons maple syrup

- 4 to 6 small acorn squash (optional)

Reminisce & Relish
Your Keepsake Recipes

Point of View
DINNER

"Full as a tick and happy as a pig in slop."

Since meeting Tres, I've seen *dinner* differently. We met at a co-worker's birthday *dinner*. Our first date was over *dinner*. It was over a sushi *dinner* that Tres learned I was a picky eater and immediately said, "we'll work on that." I met his parents over a *dinner* his dad cooked where I ate escargot for the first time. When we got engaged in San Francisco, we celebrated by going out to *dinner*. Our wedding weekend in New Orleans was celebrated over multiple fun *dinners*. Some of the best laughs we've experienced over the years have been over wine *dinners* with close friends. And, when one of us comes home stressed from a hard day, it's a relaxing *dinner* at home or an enjoyable *dinner* out where we talk about it and blow off steam. It's *dinner* we look forward to and *dinner* that makes each day extra special.

I've always heard breakfast is the most important meal of the day, but from a relationship standpoint, I just don't see it that way. Families, friends, and significant others bond over food, and usually that's sitting at the dinner table talking about life. Dinner simply brings people together the way no other meal can. One of my favorite scenes on earth is a table full of family or friends – glasses clinking, stories being told, infinite laughter – surrounded by food. Seeing pure and utter joy on every person's face around a dinner table gives me life because that very sight is a perfectly painted picture of what brings people together in celebration and what makes me love life the very most – food. Each time I see this, I'm reminded that in a world of division and conflict we can all agree that food is the centerpiece to gathering, love, and happiness.

Next time you're at a restaurant, look around. Try to find someone who looks miserable sitting with loved ones – or even colleagues – surrounded by food and wine. I bet you won't see it. What I bet you will see is celebration, radiance, and the art of why we all love food. My hope is this chapter will inspire you to make dinner the most important meal of the day. Invite friends over to sit at that long dining room table more than a few times a year, break out that nice bottle of wine you've been saving for a special occasion, eat in your backyard when the weather's nice, and take your time savoring dinner with your family each night. Eat slow, talk long, laugh hard. And make sure you get full as a tick. It'll make you happy as a pig in slop.

Ten Minute Balsamic Salmon with Tomato Avocado Salad

Serves 4

- ¾ cup good-quality balsamic vinegar
- Good-quality extra virgin olive oil
- 4 fresh, center-cut salmon fillets - skin removed
- Kosher salt and freshly ground black pepper
- 20 ounces grape tomatoes
- 2 avocados

Notes

Everyone needs a couple of quick and easy recipes to fall back on during hectic weeks. This is Tres's and my go-to. When I say we have this at least once a week, I'm not joking. I created this recipe in a hurry one night after a busy day, and ever since, it's been a staple in our house. Tres loves it so much, he will sometimes request it a second night in the same week. Any dinner that popular that only takes ten minutes is a winner in my book.

Preheat your oven to 425 degrees. Make the Balsamic Syrup. In a small saucepan, heat ½ cup of the balsamic vinegar over high heat. Bring to a slight boil then lower the heat. Simmer until slightly syrupy. Keep warm.

Make the salmon. Bring an oven-safe sauté pan with a splash of olive oil to the highest heat until the olive oil is smoking. While the pan is heating, prepare the salmon. Rub each fillet with 1 tablespoon of olive oil and sprinkle each with ½ teaspoon of salt and ¼ teaspoon of pepper. When the oil is smoking, place the salmon in the pan, top side down, and don't touch or move for 2 full minutes – not moving it creates an amazing crust. Flip the salmon and let cook for one minute on the other side, then transfer the pan to the oven for 4 minutes.

While the salmon is cooking, slice the tomatoes in half, cube the avocados, and place both in a large bowl. Toss together with two tablespoons of the olive oil, the remaining ¼ cup of the balsamic, 2 teaspoons of salt, and 1 teaspoon of pepper. Serve the salmon over a bed of the salad with a heavy drizzle of the balsamic syrup.

Flank Steak with Chimichurri Sauce over Cauliflower Purée

Serves 4 to 6

Several years ago Tres and I visited Rio de Janeiro, Brazil with some friends. To this very day, it's one of our favorite places in the world. The scenery is unlike anything I've ever seen, but we also fell in love with the food – what's not to like about steak, steak and more steak?! Meat is everywhere in Rio and the sauces they serve alongside are perfection. When I discovered how easy chimichurri was to make, I was excited to create my own at home. The cauliflower puree is a healthy substitute for garlic mashed potatoes, and both the puree and chimichurri can be made ahead for a quick, easy weeknight dinner.

Make the chimichurri sauce. In the bowl of a food processor, place the parsley, cilantro, garlic, red wine vinegar, cumin, oregano, red pepper flakes, salt, and lemon juice. Blend on high until it all comes together. Then stream in the olive oil until smooth.

🕐 *Set aside or refrigerate for up to 3 days until ready to use.*

Make the cauliflower purée. In a blender or food processor, place the steamed cauliflower, garlic, Parmesan, cream cheese, butter, salt, and pepper. Blend on high until smooth and silky.

🕐 *Keep warm in the blender or refrigerate for up to 3 days and reheat before serving.*

Make the flank steak. Heat a cast iron or grill pan over medium-high heat. Brush the flank steak with olive oil and sprinkle liberally with salt and pepper on both sides. Pan sear or grill the steak for 4 to 5 minutes on each side for medium-rare. Cover in foil and set aside for 5 minutes to rest. Slice into thin strips across the grain. Build the plates by spreading a large spoonful of cauliflower purée on the bottom of each plate. Top with the flank steak strips, then finish with a heaping spoonful of chimichurri sauce.

CHIMICHURRI SAUCE:

- ½ cup chopped parsley
- ½ cup chopped cilantro
- 3 garlic cloves – chopped
- 2 tablespoons red wine vinegar
- 2 teaspoons ground cumin
- 1 teaspoon dried oregano
- ½ teaspoon red pepper flakes
- ½ teaspoon kosher salt
- ½ lemon - juiced
- ½ cup good-quality extra virgin olive oil

CAULIFLOWER PURÉE:

- 1 small cauliflower head - cut into florets, steamed, and kept warm
- 1 garlic clove - chopped
- ¼ cup freshly grated Parmesan
- 2 tablespoons fat-free cream cheese – room temperature
- 1 ½ tablespoons unsalted butter – room temperature
- 1 teaspoon kosher salt
- ½ teaspoon freshly ground black pepper

FLANK STEAK:

- 1 (2 to 2 ½ pounds) flank steak
- Olive oil
- Kosher salt and freshly ground black pepper

149

Caribbean Seared Tuna with Mojito Sauce

Serves 4

The beach is never my first pick when planning a vacation, but the one island I will go back to multiple times without question is St. Barths in the Caribbean. The island is tiny, so the only way to get to it is by hopper plane. It's also French, so you somewhat feel like you're in France – immersed in French cuisine, an endless champagne selection, and a beautiful language. On one of our beach days, we sat under umbrellas at a little restaurant with sand under our feet, and I ordered a tuna dish that blew my mind. This dish is light but hearty with a little spice that quickly gets cooled off by the tropical, creamy mint sauce.

In a large sauté pan, heat the olive oil over medium-high heat. Sprinkle the tuna on both sides with salt. Combine the Jamaican Jerk seasoning, paprika, garlic, and cinnamon in a small bowl. Cover each side of the tuna steaks liberally with the mixture, pressing to adhere. Let sit at room temperature for at least 10 minutes.

Make the mojito sauce in a blender by combining the mango or papaya, yogurt, honey, lime zest and juice, mint, and salt. Blend at high speed until smooth. *Refrigerate for up to 3 days until ready to use.*

Sear each tuna steak for 1 to 2 minutes on each side for rare, forming a crust on each side. Transfer the tuna to a cutting board and thinly slice at an angle. Cover a plate with a thin layer of the mojito sauce. Top with the sliced tuna and a sprig of mint.

- 1 tablespoon olive oil
- 4 (6-ounce each) good-quality tuna steaks
- Kosher salt
- 2 tablespoons Jamaican Jerk seasoning
- 1 tablespoon smoked paprika
- ½ teaspoon granulated garlic
- ¼ teaspoon ground cinnamon
- 2 medium ripe mangos or papayas – peeled, cored, and chopped
- ⅓ cup plain or vanilla Greek yogurt
- ¼ cup honey
- 1 lime – zested and juiced
- 1 large handful of mint – chopped, plus more for garnish

Notes

....
....
....
....
....

Prosciutto Wrapped Tenderloin with Fig Glaze

When Tres and I first started dating, we would go out for dinner nearly every weeknight. That was before my cooking days, plus we were younger with a lot more energy back then. I'm not saying we aren't just as fun now as we used to be, but after a long day of work we prefer to cook at home and take it easy, saving our go-out nights for the weekends. We still like our meals at home to be just as enjoyable as a night out on the town, so I usually try to cook something restaurant-quality but simple. This is the ideal dinner for a fancy night in – easy, delectable, and perfect with a nice bottle of wine.

Preheat your oven to 450 degrees. Rinse the pork and pat dry with paper towels. If there's excess fat on the pork, trim it off and discard. Line a baking sheet with parchment paper and place the pork on top. Sprinkle liberally on all sides with salt and pepper. Then add the rosemary and thyme, pressing to adhere.

Working with one piece of prosciutto at a time, wrap the loins with each slice, starting at one end and working your way to the other end. Lay each slice over the top and tuck the ends under. In a small bowl, mix together the fig jam, balsamic vinegar, Dijon mustard, and lemon juice. Spoon the mixture over the prosciutto. Roast for about 15 to 20 minutes for 1 pound loins and 20 to 25 minutes for a 2 pound loin – or until a meat thermometer reads 145 degrees. Remove from the oven, cover in foil, and let rest for about 10 minutes before slicing.

Serves 4

- 2 pounds pork tenderloin (1 large or 2 small)
- 2 teaspoons kosher salt
- 1 teaspoon freshly ground black pepper
- 2 teaspoons fresh rosemary – minced
- 1 teaspoon fresh thyme - minced
- 8 to 10 slices prosciutto, about 4 ounces
- 2 tablespoons fig jam
- 1 teaspoon balsamic vinegar
- ½ teaspoon Dijon mustard
- Squeeze of lemon

Notes

Spring Chicken

Growing up in the country, I can remember spring being a vibrant, colorful time of year. Mama loved her flowers and always planted new beautiful ones each new spring. Living so far away from the city, the smell of spring was so vivid and the grass was so bright. I remember riding bikes outside until dark, playing in the woods all day and exploring. We grew up on ten acres of land with neighbors who lived on even more land, so there was a lot to discover. This chicken was inspired by the beautiful green and floral colors of spring in Mississippi and takes me right back to those carefree days.

Preheat your oven to 350 degrees. In a small bowl, mix together the butter, garlic, and thyme. Set aside. In another bowl, mix together the lemon zest, orange zest, dill, chives, and parsley. Set aside. Pat the chicken breasts dry on all sides using paper towels and then place on a baking sheet, skin side up. Without tearing the skin off the chicken, using your fingers, lift the skin up and rub 1 tablespoon of the butter mixture under the skin and on the tops of each breast.

Liberally salt and pepper both sides of the chicken then drizzle about ½ tablespoon of olive oil over the skin. Sprinkle about ¼ of the citrus-herb mixture over the tops. Bake for about 30 to 40 minutes, or until the thickest part of the breast reads 165 degrees. Turn your oven setting to broil, and broil the chicken for 3 to 5 minutes, or until crispy. Plate and sprinkle with the remaining citrus-herb mixture. Garnish with orange and lemon slices.

Serves 4

- 4 tablespoons unsalted butter – room temperature
- 1 tablespoon finely minced garlic
- 1 ½ teaspoons minced fresh thyme
- Zest of 1 large lemon
- Zest of 1 large orange
- ⅓ cup minced fresh dill
- ¼ cup minced fresh chives
- 2 tablespoons minced parsley
- 4 bone-in, skin-on chicken breasts
- 2 tablespoons olive oil
- Kosher salt and freshly ground black pepper
- Orange and lemon slices – for garnish

Notes

Coffee Rubbed Filet

When I became a coffee drinker, I simply started enjoying life more. As a coffee drinker, you look forward to getting up early. You savor sitting in silence, wrapped up in a blanket on cozy mornings. You appreciate the cold and the rain more because there's a cup of coffee to warm you. And nothing beats conversation with a family member or a friend with two "Cups of Joe" between you. Plus, the jolt of caffeine doesn't hurt either. When I'm not drinking coffee, I experiment in the kitchen with it. This coffee rubbed filet is strong and warm yet spicy and sweet. Cooking it on the grill makes it smoky and extra flavorful.

Heat a grill or grill pan over high heat. Take the steaks out of the fridge and let them come to room temperature, about 20 minutes. In a medium bowl, make the dry rub by mixing together the brown sugar, coffee grinds, smoked salt, garlic, paprika, red pepper flakes, cinnamon, and black pepper. Brush the steaks lightly with the melted butter and generously rub them with a thick layer of the coffee mixture on all sides.

Grill the steaks for about 6 minutes per side (or until a meat thermometer reads 135 degrees) for medium-rare. When finished grilling, set the steaks aside with foil tented over the top of them for 10 minutes before cutting into them. These are best served with Truffle Duck Fat Fries (page 89).

Notes

....

....

....

Serves 4

- 4 (1 ½-inch thick) filet mignons
- ½ cup light brown sugar
- ¼ cup ground coffee
- 1 tablespoon smoked salt (or kosher)
- 2 teaspoons granulated garlic
- 2 teaspoons paprika
- 2 teaspoons red pepper flakes
- 1 teaspoon ground cinnamon
- ½ teaspoon freshly ground black pepper
- 2 tablespoons unsalted butter - melted

Brown Sugar Short Ribs

The best holiday recipes are family heirlooms that have been passed down for years. There's something familiar and warm about them that make you feel like a kid again. Some seem so sacred, you feel an obligation to keep them top secret. That recipe for me is my Mammaw's Holiday Ravioli, a recipe passed down for generations. Because I will forever keep that recipe to myself and close family, I decided to come up with a holiday recipe of my own that I could share with friends and blog readers – these rich, slightly sweet short ribs. I serve them alongside the Holiday Ravioli every Christmas dinner and now have my own recipe to add to the family cookbook. This dish is also the one I used when auditioning for *MasterChef* Season Six where I was chosen as a Top One Hundred Contestant, so it's also been TV-approved.

Preheat your oven to 350 degrees. In a Dutch oven or large cast iron pot, heat the olive oil over medium-high heat. Sprinkle the short ribs liberally with salt and pepper. Sear all sides of the short ribs until browned and a nice crust is formed. Set aside on a plate.

Turn the heat down to medium, add the onion, and cook until slightly brown. Add the garlic and cook for one minute, or until fragrant. Deglaze the pan with the red wine and scrape up all brown bits from the bottom. Let the wine reduce by half. Add the beef stock, tomato paste, bay leaves, and stir together.

Place the ribs back into the pot, making sure they're almost covered in the liquid but you can still see the tops. If they need more liquid, add more stock. Sprinkle the rosemary, thyme, and brown sugar over the ribs. Roast in the oven for 2 ½ to 3 hours, or until tender and almost falling off the bone. Transfer the ribs to a serving platter. Skim and discard the fat off the top of the gravy then blend what's left with a hand-held blender – if you don't have one, you can use a regular blender or leave the sauce chunky. Serve gravy atop the ribs or on the side.

Serves 4

- 2 tablespoons olive oil
- 4 to 5 pounds short ribs
- Kosher salt and freshly ground black pepper
- 1 large onion – diced
- 4 garlic cloves – minced
- 1 ½ cups good red wine
- 3 cups beef stock, plus more if needed
- 2 tablespoons tomato paste
- 2 bay leaves
- 2 teaspoons fresh rosemary
- 2 teaspoons fresh thyme
- ½ cup light brown sugar

Notes

Christmas Fettuccine

I'd never heard of Christmas Fettuccine or knew it was a thing until watching the movie "The Holiday." That movie has forever been in my Christmas movie rotation, and since the first time I saw it, I've craved Fettuccine Alfredo around the holidays. I wanted to come up with the perfect recipe for it, and decided I couldn't make it a common Alfredo sauce - it must have holiday flavors. The addition of allspice and mint make this pasta one of a kind and Santa approved.

Make the pasta. Dump the all-purpose flour and semolina flour into a mound on a clean work surface. Using a fork, mix the two together, then make a hole in the center of the mound with your hand. Crack the whole eggs and egg yolks into the center and add the olive oil and salt. Beat the eggs, olive oil, and salt together with the fork until smooth. Slowly start adding the mounded flour to the wet mixture with the fork. Add several tablespoons of water to help it come together, then begin kneading. If it gets too wet, add more flour; too dry, add more water. Knead for 5 to 8 minutes, or until dough becomes smooth.

🕐 *Wrap the dough ball in plastic wrap and refrigerate for at least 30 minutes or overnight.*

When ready to roll out, cut the dough into quarters and shape each into a flat, rectangular disk. Using a pasta rolling machine, run each dough quarter through until about 1/8-inch thick, then run through the fettuccine attachment to make the noodles. If you don't have a pasta machine, use a rolling pin. Roll the dough out as thin as you can, keeping a rectangular shape, then use a sharp knife to cut the noodles into strips. Flour a sheet pan and place the noodles on the pan until ready to boil.

Make the sauce. In a large sauté pan, melt the butter and heavy cream together over medium-low heat. Add the garlic, allspice, nutmeg, and a sprinkle of salt and pepper. Let cook for at least one minute, then keep warm over low heat.

In a pot of boiling salted water, cook the pasta for 2 minutes. Drain, reserving the pasta cooking water. Then immediately transfer the pasta to the heated sauce. Add at least ¼ cup of pasta water, the Parmesan, and the chopped mint in with the sauce. Toss everything together and serve with a sprinkle more of Parmesan and chopped mint.

Serves 4

PASTA:

- 2 cups all-purpose flour, plus more for dusting
- 1 cup semolina flour
- 2 whole large eggs
- 3 egg yolks
- 1 teaspoon olive oil
- Dash kosher salt, plus more for boiling

SAUCE:

- ½ stick unsalted butter
- 1 cup heavy cream
- 3 garlic cloves - sliced thin by mandoline (about 1/8-inch thick)
- ½ teaspoon allspice
- ¼ teaspoon freshly grated nutmeg
- Kosher salt and freshly ground black pepper
- Freshly grated Parmesan
- ¼ cup chopped mint, plus more for garnish

Notes

Farmer's Market Pasta

Serves 4 to 6

When I first started experimenting with my own recipes, Mama and I went to my hometown farmer's market one Saturday to get the creative juices flowing. My parents still live in the town where I grew up, Hernando, Mississippi. This little suburb is charming and the town square farmer's market is complete inspiration. That day I found squash, eggplant and tomatoes. I knew I wanted to roast them, and mama had bacon in the fridge and pasta in the pantry, so I went to work. When it was finished, Mama and Pop both said it was the best pasta they'd ever had. Thank goodness, I wrote the recipe down that day.

Preheat your oven to 450 degrees. Fry the bacon, drain on a paper towel-lined plate, and retain the grease. Spread the veggie cubes on a baking sheet. Toss together with bacon grease, olive oil, garlic, salt, and pepper. Roast in the oven for 15 to 20 minutes, or until golden and softened. While the veggies roast, cook the pasta in a large pot of boiling salted water according to the package directions, or until al dente.

In a medium bowl, combine the lemon juice, vinegar, garlic, Dijon mustard, salt, and pepper. Whisk in the olive oil. Spoon the cooked pasta directly into a serving bowl with a couple tablespoons of pasta water. Add the bacon, Parmesan, roasted veggies and all their juices, and the dressing. Toss together to combine. Top with more Parmesan and chopped basil.

Notes

....

....

....

PASTA:

- 4 slices of thick-cut bacon – sliced thin
- 3 pounds fresh veggies (such as eggplant, squash, zucchini, tomatoes) – cut into 1-inch cubes
- 1 tablespoon olive oil
- 3 garlic cloves – minced
- 1 ½ teaspoons kosher salt
- 1 teaspoon freshly ground black pepper
- 1 pound penne (or any bite-sized pasta)
- ½ cup freshly grated Parmesan cheese, plus more for garnish
- ¼ cup chopped fresh basil, plus more for garnish

DRESSING:

- ½ lemon – juiced
- 2 tablespoons red wine vinegar
- 1 tablespoon minced garlic
- 1 tablespoon Dijon mustard
- ½ teaspoon kosher salt
- ¼ teaspoon freshly ground black pepper
- ½ cup good-quality extra virgin olive oil

Beef Stew over Polenta

I think we all make the mistake sometimes of feeling like we can't have people over unless our home is immaculate, and the meal we serve has been fussed over all day. When I first started entertaining, I was the world's worst at this and would often forgo fixing myself up in order to have a perfectly spotless house and intricate meal for my guests. I remember telling one of my girlfriends, I may look horrific tonight, but I'll be damned if my house isn't perfect and dinner isn't flawless. Over the years, I have realized that's not what a gathering is all about and your guests don't care. The best parties I've had were unplanned, my house wasn't immaculate, and the food was an easy, throw in the oven and forget it meal. Remember that next time you invite guests over – you'll notice company feels more welcome in an easy-going atmosphere. Make this beef stew – it's casual, welcoming, and fuss-free.

Preheat your oven to 325 degrees. In a large Dutch oven or pot, heat the olive oil over medium-high heat. Pat the stew meat dry with paper towels. In a bowl, combine the ¾ cup of flour, ½ tablespoon salt, and ½ tablespoon of pepper. Toss the meat into the mixture, shake off the excess, and sear the meat until browned on all sides. Transfer the browned meat to a plate.

Fry the bacon in the pot until crispy and then transfer to the plate with the meat. Place the onions, parsnips, carrots, and sweet potatoes into the pot. Season with a dash of salt and cook for about 10 to 12 minutes, or until softened. Add the mushrooms, garlic, and another dash of salt and cook for about 2 more minutes. Pour in the brandy to deglaze the pot, scraping the brown bits off the bottom, and let it reduce by half. Pour in the wine, beef stock, and Worcestershire sauce. Put the meat back in and add the rosemary and bay leaf. Turn the heat to high and let come to a boil for one minute. Put the lid on the pot and transfer to the oven. Cook for 2 hours, or until meat is tender and shreds easily. In a small bowl, combine the remaining 2 tablespoons of flour and the remaining 2 tablespoons of butter (from the polenta). Stir the paste into the finished stew.

🕑 *The stew can be cooked and refrigerated for 3 to 4 days or frozen for 3 months and reheated.*

While the stew is still in the oven, about 30 minutes before serving, make the polenta. In a large saucepan, heat 4 cups of water and 1 teaspoon of salt over high heat. When the water comes to a boil, slowly whisk in the polenta. Let boil for 1 to 2 minutes, constantly whisking. Turn the heat down to low, cover the pot, and let cook for 20 to 25 minutes, uncovering and whisking occasionally. Similar to grits, the polenta should be a creamy – not too watery, not too dry – consistency. Take off the heat and stir in the Parmesan cheese and 2 tablespoons of the butter. Taste and add more salt if needed. To serve, ladle a small serving of polenta into a bowl and top with the stew. Garnish with parsley if desired.

Notes

Serves 4 to 6

- 1 tablespoon olive oil
- 2 pounds beef chuck or stew meat cut into 1-inch pieces
- ¾ cup all-purpose flour, plus 2 tablespoons
- Kosher salt and freshly ground black pepper
- 6 ounces thick-cut bacon - cut into strips
- 2 onions – roughly chopped
- 2 small parsnips - peeled and chopped into 1-inch pieces
- 4 large carrots - peeled and cut diagonally into 1-inch pieces
- 1 cup sweet potatoes - chopped into 1-inch cubes
- 8 ounces white button mushrooms - sliced
- 3 garlic cloves - minced
- ¼ cup brandy
- 1 bottle red wine
- 2 cups beef stock
- 2 tablespoons Worcestershire sauce
- 2 sprigs fresh rosemary
- 1 bay leaf
- 1 cup polenta
- ½ cup freshly grated Parmesan
- 4 tablespoons unsalted butter - room temperature
- Parsley (optional)

Homemade Ricotta Ravioli with Brown Butter Sage Sauce

Serves 4 to 6

The first time I made my Mammaw's famous Holiday Ravioli I didn't cook and had zero kitchen tools, but I was craving her ravioli and was determined to have it. When it was time to roll out the dough, I realized I didn't have a rolling pin. I almost threw my hands up and quit but suddenly noticed a wine bottle on the counter - my problem was solved! Yes, I used a wine bottle to roll out my first pasta dough. Moral of the story – wine solves everything, and I've come a long way in the kitchen. Mammaw's ravioli dough is plump and dumpling-like, making it easy to roll with a bottle. This particular dough recipe is different but just as delectable – passed through a pasta machine, it's extra-thin, delicate, and somewhat feminine. The homemade ricotta makes each bite-sized piece like a fluffy cloud in your mouth.

In a large Dutch oven or cast-iron pot, place the milk, cream, and salt. Stir together over medium heat. Let the mixture come to a complete boil, stirring occasionally, for about 5 minutes. Turn off the heat and stir in the vinegar. Let the mixture sit for at least 6 to 7 minutes, or until it curdles. There will be large chunks throughout the mixture. Set a large sieve, covered with a damp cheesecloth, over a deep bowl. Pour the milk mixture into the sieve, and let the excess liquid drip into the bowl.

Occasionally discarding the liquid in the bottom of the bowl, let the mixture sit at room temperature for 30 to 45 minutes, or until it's thick with very little liquid - the longer it sits, the thicker it gets. When it's nice and thick, pour into a bowl, add 1 tablespoon of olive oil, and stir to combine.

🕐 *Cover and refrigerate the ricotta until ready to use for up to 5 days.*

HOMEMADE RICOTTA:

- 1 quart whole milk
- 2 cups heavy cream
- 1 ¼ teaspoons kosher salt
- 3 tablespoons white wine vinegar or lemon juice
- Good-quality extra virgin olive oil

RAVIOLI:

- 1 cup cake flour
- 1 cup all-purpose flour
- 3 large egg yolks
- ¼ teaspoon kosher salt
- ¼ cup extra virgin olive oil
- Egg wash, for brushing

BROWN BUTTER SAGE SAUCE:

- 1 stick unsalted butter
- 20 sage leaves
- Freshly grated Parmesan cheese
- Fleur de sel (or flaky sea salt)

Recipe continues on next page.

Homemade Ricotta Ravioli with
Brown Butter Sage Sauce *(cont.)*

Dump the cake flour and all-purpose flour in a mound on a clean work surface. Using a fork, mix the two together, and then make a well in the center with your hand. Place the egg yolks, salt, and olive oil in the center of the well and beat together with a fork until smooth. Slowly begin bringing the flour into the egg mixture, adding 1 tablespoon of water at a time to moisten the dough. Continue to bring the flour into the dough, adding water as needed. Once all the flour is somewhat mixed in, bring the dough together with your hands and begin kneading. If it gets too wet, add more flour; too dry, add more water – it should be firm and smooth but not sticky. Knead for 5 to 8 minutes, or until the dough becomes a firm, even ball.

🕐 *Cover in plastic wrap and refrigerate for at least 30 minutes or overnight.*

When ready to use, cut the dough ball into four equal parts. Working with each piece of dough, one at a time, form into a thin, rectangular disk. Then run each piece through a pasta rolling machine, starting with the thickest setting. Continue to run the dough through several times, adjusting the setting each time until the pasta is about 1/8 to 1/16-inch thick.

Working one at a time, lay the rectangular pasta sheets out. Starting from one end, spoon about 1 teaspoon of ricotta in the middle of the sheet and continue to the end of the sheet, spacing each spoonful about 1 inch apart. Brush the egg wash around the edges of the sheet and in between each spoonful of ricotta. Fold the dough over, long-ways, and press around each filling to remove air bubbles. Using a biscuit cutter, cut out the raviolis into half-moon shapes and use a fork to crimp the edges. In a pot of boiling salted water, cook the ravioli for 2 to 3 minutes.

🕐 *The ravioli can also be frozen – spaced out and flat – in plastic bags for up to 3 months.*

In a medium sauté pan, heat the butter over medium-low heat. When it starts to brown, add the sage and cook until the sage is crispy and the butter is brown and nutty, about 3 to 5 minutes. When ready to serve, plate the cooked ravioli, spoon the sauce over with the sage leaves, freshly grate a thick layer of Parmesan over the top, and a sprinkle of fleur de sel to finish.

Notes

....

....

Bison Bolognese

To country folks, "spaghetti" isn't a type of pasta – it's a complete dish with cooked noodles and meat sauce. At least growing up in my house, that's what we called it. When we heard Mama say, "we're having spaghetti for dinner," we knew that meant noodles and sauce. And Spaghetti Night was one of our favorite nights. It was literally not until I started cooking and traveled to Italy that I learned "spaghetti" is a pasta noodle, and the meat sauce that goes on top is called Bolognese. Whatever. I'm from Mississippi and don't care what you choose to call it. I'm just here to tell you, this is the best version of that childhood classic you've ever eaten!

Heat a large Dutch oven or pot over medium-low heat. Add 1 tablespoon of olive oil and the bacon, and fry until crispy. Add the onion, celery, carrots, mushrooms, and garlic. Season with 1 teaspoon of salt and a dash of pepper. Cook for about 35 minutes, or until the veggies are slightly brown, stirring occasionally.

Increase the heat to medium-high and add the bison. Season with a heavy dash of salt and pepper, and cook, breaking the meat up into small pieces, until browned. Deglaze the pot with the red wine, scraping the brown bits from the bottom. Add the milk, tomato paste, and tomatoes. Bring the sauce to a slight boil; then lower the temperature to medium-low. Add the Parmesan rind and simmer for at least 2 hours. The longer the sauce simmers, the better it tastes - I like to make mine in the morning and let it simmer all day.

About 30 minutes before serving, place ¼ cup of the olive oil, the basil leaves, and red pepper flakes in a small saucepan and warm the mixture over low heat. Once warm, set aside and let steep for about 30 minutes. Strain the infused oil directly into the sauce and discard the basil and red pepper flakes. Add the parsley, chopped basil, Parmesan cheese, and butter to the sauce and stir to combine. Season the sauce with salt and pepper, tasting the sauce as you salt and pepper to get the flavor just right. Serve over cooked bucatini.

Notes

....

....

....

This recipe makes a huge batch of sauce. Luckily, it freezes perfectly for up to 3 months, and I happen to think it tastes even better after it's been frozen.

Serves 10 to 12

- Extra virgin olive oil
- 5 slices thick-cut bacon - diced small
- 1 large onion - diced small
- 1 large celery stick - diced small
- 1 large carrot – peeled and diced small
- 8 ounces baby bella mushrooms – diced small
- 3 garlic cloves - minced
- Kosher salt and freshly ground black pepper
- 2 pounds ground bison
- 1 ½ cups red wine
- 1 cup whole milk
- 6 ounces tomato paste
- 42 ounces San Marzano whole peeled tomatoes - crushed by hand
- 1 large Parmesan rind
- 10 basil leaves, plus 3 tablespoons chopped
- 1 teaspoon red pepper flakes
- ¼ cup parsley - chopped
- ½ cup grated Parmesan, plus extra for serving
- 4 tablespoons unsalted butter
- 2 pounds bucatini pasta – cooked

Roasted Red Snapper with White Balsamic Tomatoes

Tres spends a great deal of his time traveling for work, but luckily, he works with a lot of good friends and sometimes the wives get to come along. One trip we make every year is an event on the Gulf Coast in Florida. Several years ago, I found a local fish market, cooked for the entire group, and it's been expected of me ever since. The Gulf's red snapper is fresh, flaky and beyond delish, so it's always a go-to dinner item to cook when we're there. This version is my favorite – all done in a foil packet so it's easy but so good, no one knows how easy. Even the kids' plates are clean when I cook this one.

Preheat your oven to 400 degrees. Place each snapper fillet on a large piece of aluminum foil. Season both sides with salt and pepper. Fold the sides of the foil up to make a shallow bowl around each filet, and place on a baking sheet.

In a large bowl, mix together the tomatoes, basil, balsamic reduction, garlic, red pepper flakes, 1 teaspoon salt, and ½ teaspoon pepper. Spoon the tomato mixture over each fillet, completely covering the fish. Add about 2 tablespoons of white wine and drizzle 1 tablespoon of olive oil over each fillet. Fold the sides of the foil up to close, making a package but leaving a small opening in the top. Bake the fish for 15 to 20 minutes, or until it flakes. Serve each fillet on a plate with the tomato mixture and juices on top. Top each piece with extra basil and a drizzle of olive oil.

Serves 4

- 4 (6 to 8-ounce each) fresh snapper fillets
- Kosher salt and freshly ground black pepper
- 2 pounds plum tomatoes - chopped
- 2 cups fresh basil - chopped, plus extra for garnish
- ¼ cup white balsamic reduction
- 3 garlic cloves - minced
- ½ teaspoon red pepper flakes
- ½ cup white wine
- ¼ cup good-quality extra virgin olive oil, plus more for drizzling

Notes

Cocoa Cola Baby Back Ribs

Serves 4

Memphis in May World Championship Barbecue Cooking Contest – a.k.a. "BBQ Fest" to locals – is arguably the biggest, most exciting week in the Bluff City. Tents line Tom Lee Park on the Mississippi River where people are ready to compete, eat and party. It's really something unique to see, and I tell all my out of town friends that if they're going to visit Memphis, this is the week to do it. We typically have friends stay with us, so I wanted something I could make every year as a welcome treat and introduction to the festival. These baby backs are slightly chocolaty from the cocoa with a hint of sweetness from the cola, but they're overall savory and finger licking good – inspired by the best BBQ in the world.

- 2 racks baby back ribs
- 4 tablespoons unsweetened cocoa powder
- 3 tablespoons light brown sugar
- 2 tablespoons kosher salt
- 2 teaspoons liquid smoke
- 2 teaspoons allspice
- 1 teaspoon smoked paprika
- ½ teaspoon freshly ground black pepper
- 1½ cups regular cola
- 4 medium onions - roughly chopped into large pieces
- 1 cup good-quality barbecue sauce

Rinse the ribs and pat dry with paper towels. In a small bowl, mix together the cocoa, brown sugar, salt, liquid smoke, allspice, paprika, and pepper. Rub the mixture onto the ribs and press to adhere.

🕐 *Cover the ribs and refrigerate for a few hours or overnight.*

Preheat your oven to 325 degrees. Prep two baking pans by pouring ¾ cup of cola into each pan. Place the chopped onions over the cola and place the ribs on top of the onions. Cover the pan tightly with foil. Bake for 2 ½ to 3 hours, or until meat is tender and almost falling off the bone. I like my ribs to still have substance to them – not quite falling off the bone.

Using tongs, move the ribs to a baking sheet lined with foil. Strain the onions from the cola. Reserve ¼ cup of the cola and mix with the barbecue sauce. Brush a thick layer of the sauce onto the ribs. Put the ribs back in the oven for 20 minutes. Serve with the extra cola-barbecue sauce on the side.

Notes

....
....
....
....
....

Spaghetti with Mascarpone Marinara and Pork Crunchies

I discovered my love for cooking when I was in graduate school. Between classes, writing papers and studying, my life was spent learning about food, reading cookbooks, watching cooking television and creating my own recipes. I became obsessed, and decided as soon as I graduated, I would start my recipe blog. The very day I got my diploma, I cooked a big lunch for my family and posted my first recipe – this spaghetti dish. Years later, this dish is still one of my favorites to serve at dinner parties and my number one seller when catering for my personal chef business. One of my biggest accomplishments in life was getting my master's degree but so was starting my blog with this exact recipe. If you're wondering what a pork crunchie is, make this dish, and you'll discover it's one of the best bites of food you'll ever eat.

Preheat your oven to 325 degrees. Line 2 large baking sheets with foil and spread the salami slices on one and pepperoni slices on the other. Bake for 8 to 10 minutes, or until crisp – watch carefully so they don't burn. Let cool, crumble into a bowl, and set aside.

In a large sauté pan, heat the olive oil over medium-high heat. Add the onion and a dash of salt and pepper. Cook until slightly brown, about 5 to 7 minutes. Turn the heat down to medium-low, and add the garlic, thyme, oregano, and red pepper flakes. Then cook for two more minutes. Pour in the wine, scraping brown bits from the bottom of the pan, and let the sauce reduce by half. Stir in the marinara and mascarpone until the cheese is melted and the sauce is heated through. Add 1 ½ teaspoon of salt or more to taste.

🕐 *Sauce can be refrigerated for up 5 days or frozen for up to 3 months.*

In a large pot of boiling salted water, cook the spaghetti according to package directions or until al dente. Transfer the spaghetti to a bowl and toss together with half the sauce, basil, Parmesan, and at least ¼ cup pasta water. Top with the remaining sauce, crunchies, and a sprinkle of basil and Parmesan.

Notes

Serves 4 to 6

- 1 (4-ounce) package large pepperoni slices
- 1 (4-ounce) package large salami slices
- 1 tablespoon olive oil
- 1 small onion – diced
- Kosher salt and freshly ground black pepper
- 3 garlic cloves – minced
- 2 teaspoons fresh thyme – minced
- 1 teaspoon dried oregano
- ½ teaspoon red pepper flakes
- ¼ cup red wine
- 1 (24-ounce) jar marinara sauce
- 1 (8-ounce) container mascarpone
- 1 pound spaghetti
- ¼ cup fresh basil – chopped, plus more for garnish
- ¼ cup freshly grated Parmesan, plus more for garnish

Low-Fat Poppy Seed Chicken Quinoa Casserole

If there's anything a Southern woman could make one hundred killer versions of - it's a casserole. You name the casserole and as Southern women, we've cooked it, we've eaten it and we've scrapped the bottom of the pan because every last bite was delicious. When I was in college, Poppy Seed Chicken, was a favorite of mine. This is the healthy version of that exact dish – with low fat, lower-carbs, and with protein packed healthy quinoa.

Preheat your oven to 350 degrees. In a large bowl, mix together the shredded chicken and quinoa. Set aside. Heat a large sauté pan with the olive oil over medium-low heat. Add the shallot, garlic, mushrooms and salt. Stir together until the mushrooms start to wilt. Add the marsala and sauté a few more minutes until the mushrooms are soft.

Pour the mushroom mixture into the bowl with the chicken and quinoa. Add the cream of mushroom soup, sour cream, and poppy seeds. Season with pepper. Stir together until completely combined. Taste for seasoning and add more salt and pepper if needed. Pour the mixture into 4 small ramekins (or an 8-inch casserole dish) and top with the cracker crumbs, butter or olive oil, and a sprinkle of the poppy seeds. Bake for 20 to 25 minutes, or until golden and bubbly.

Serves 4

- 1 whole smoked (or rotisserie) chicken - skin removed, meat shredded
- 1 cup cooked quinoa
- 1 tablespoon olive oil
- 1 shallot - sliced
- 3 garlic cloves - minced
- 2 (8-ounce) packages mushrooms - sliced
- 1 teaspoon kosher salt, plus more to taste
- 2 tablespoons Marsala cooking wine
- 2 (10.5-ounce)cans low-fat cream of mushroom soup
- ⅔ cup fat-free sour cream
- 2 tablespoons poppy seeds, plus more for sprinkling
- Freshly ground black pepper
- 12 reduced-fat, butter-flavored crackers - crushed
- ½ tablespoon melted unsalted butter or olive oil

Notes

....

....

....

....

....

....

Lavender Buttered Mussels over Angel Hair

Serves 4 to 6

When I auditioned for *MasterChef*, I met the loveliest gal, Keshia, who had driven to Memphis from Nashville for the tryout. As soon as we started chatting, we were instant friends and have kept in touch over the years. She has visited me a few times in Memphis, and when she comes to town, we plan party themes and menus, we play with ingredients in the kitchen and write new recipes and we eat, eat, and eat some more. I love spending time with her in the kitchen, as we have a similar cooking style – unique ingredients, fresh and seasonal foods and a fun, feminine touch to our recipes. She loves the cuisine of France as much as I do. So one year, she came in town for Bastille Day and we celebrated over a spread Julia Child would more than appreciate. I made these lavender buttered mussels, and they've been in my French cooking rotation ever since.

- 2 pounds mussels (or clams)
- Kosher salt
- 8 tablespoons unsalted butter
- 2 shallots – minced
- 3 garlic cloves – minced
- 1 tablespoon dried lavender leaves – crushed, plus more for garnish
- ½ cup white wine
- ½ lemon – zested and juiced
- 1 tablespoon chopped fresh parsley, plus more for garnish
- Freshly ground black pepper
- 1 pound angel hair pasta
- ¼ cup good-quality extra virgin olive oil, plus more for drizzling

Soak the mussels for about 10 minutes in cold water. Drain and lightly scrub the outside of the mussels with a dish brush to make sure the grit has been removed. Bring a large pot of salted water to a boil for the pasta.

Heat the butter in a large sauté pan over medium-low heat. Add the shallots, garlic, and lavender and sauté for one minute, being sure to not burn the garlic. Add the mussels and wine, cover the pot, and cook for 7 to 8 minutes, or until most mussels have opened. Discard any unopened mussels. Add the lemon zest, lemon juice, parsley, ½ teaspoon of salt, and ¼ teaspoon of pepper and stir to combine.

Cook the pasta until al dente – about 3 minutes. Drain and place in the pan with the mussels. Add the olive oil and toss together. Taste for seasoning and add more salt and pepper if needed. Serve directly from the pan or pour in a large serving bowl. Garnish with a drizzle of olive oil and a sprinkle of parsley and lavender leaves.

Notes

Autumn Roasted Chicken over Brussels Barley Salad

Serves 4

There are a million ways to roast chicken and because I love the flavors of fall, it was imperative I come up with a version for my favorite season. This recipe is an easy, super-healthy weeknight meal that heats up perfectly for lunch the next day – if you have leftovers.

Make the chicken. Preheat your oven to 400 degrees. Place the chicken tenderloins on a baking sheet covered in foil. Rub the chicken with the olive oil and sprinkle with salt and pepper on all sides. In a small bowl, mix together the orange zest, brown sugar, cinnamon, garlic, and rosemary. Rub the mixture on all sides of the chicken breasts. Roast for about 15 to 20 minutes, or until cooked through and your meat thermometer reads at least 165 degrees. Cover in foil and let rest.

Make the salad. Heat the olive oil in a sauté pan over medium heat. Sauté the Brussels sprouts with a dash of salt and pepper until crispy. In a large bowl, whisk together the Dijonnaise, olive oil, honey, and orange juice. Add the crispy Brussels and cooked barley to the bowl and stir to combine, tossing until covered in the dressing. Serve chicken on top of the salad.

Notes

....

....

....

CHICKEN:
- 1 ½ pounds chicken tenderloins
- 1 tablespoon olive oil
- 1 ½ teaspoons kosher salt
- 1 teaspoon freshly ground black pepper
- 4 teaspoons orange zest
- 1 ½ tablespoons light brown sugar
- 2 teaspoons ground cinnamon
- 2 teaspoons minced garlic
- 1 teaspoon minced rosemary

SALAD:
- 1 tablespoon olive oil
- 2 cups thinly sliced Brussels sprouts
- Kosher salt and freshly ground black pepper
- 2 tablespoons Dijonnaise
- 2 tablespoons olive oil
- 1 tablespoon honey
- 1 tablespoon orange juice
- 1 cup of cooked barley

Barley can be cooked ahead and stored in an air-tight container in the refrigerator for up to 4 days. Cook an extra-large batch at the beginning of the week and add it to salads, soups, and breakfast bowls.

Smoked Fish Pot Pie

Serves 4 to 6

I already know what you're thinking – you just read the name of this recipe and thought, eww. But you're wrong. I agree, the first thought of fish pot pie probably doesn't have your mouth watering, but I'm here to tell you, it's absolutely divine. When traveling, I always make a point to try the native land's most popular dishes and when in Scotland, I kept seeing fish pot pie on the menus. I love pot pies and I love smoked fish, so I gave it a whirl. It was one of the best, most unique dishes I'd ever eaten and I scraped my bowl clean. There's nothing to not like: mashed potatoes, smoked fish and creamy, cheesy goodness make up this pie and it's a crowd-pleaser. Be adventurous, make it. You won't be sorry.

Preheat your oven to 425 degrees. Place the potatoes in a medium saucepan and cover with water. Boil over high heat until tender and then drain. Transfer the potatoes back into the pan and add 2 tablespoons of the butter, ¼ cup of milk, 1 tablespoon of salt, and ½ tablespoon pepper. Mash together until thoroughly combined and smooth. Set aside.

In a large saucepan over medium heat, add the remaining 2 tablespoons of butter and the green onions. Cook the onions until coated in butter and slightly softened, about 2 minutes. Sprinkle in the flour and cook for another minute. Slowly whisk in the remaining 1 ½ cups milk until smooth. Let come to a slight boil, then lower the heat and simmer until thick enough to coat the back of a spoon. Remove from the heat and add the smoked fish, Gouda, Dijon mustard, chives, dill, 1 tablespoon of salt, and ½ teaspoon pepper. Mix together until combined. Transfer to an 8-inch baking dish, spoon the mashed potato mixture evenly over the top, and lightly drizzle with olive oil. Bake for about 25 to 30 minutes, or until golden. Garnish with chives.

- 2 ½ pounds russet potatoes – peeled and cut into cubes
- 4 tablespoons unsalted butter, divided
- 1 ¾ cups whole milk, divided
- Kosher salt and freshly ground black pepper
- 3 green onions, white and green parts - sliced
- 2 tablespoons all-purpose flour
- 8 ounces smoked haddock, salmon, or trout – flaked into small pieces
- 1 cup freshly grated smoked Gouda
- 2 tablespoons Dijon mustard
- 2 tablespoons sliced chives, plus more for garnish
- 1 tablespoon minced fresh dill
- Olive oil

Notes

Reminisce & Relish
Your Keepsake Recipes

Happily Ever After
DESSERT

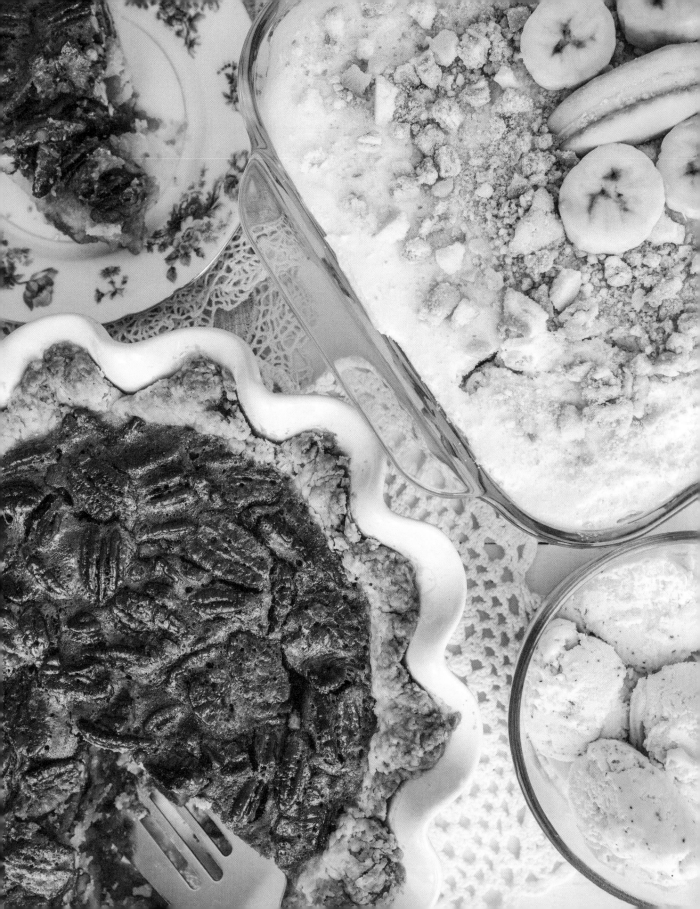

"I'm bursting, I love you so much."

Most chefs will tell you their love for cooking started at a young age with a parent or grandparent – mine started late in life with my husband. Tres is more than just my best friend and soul mate, who I've dedicated my life to – he had a significant influence on my passion for food. When we met, I was an extremely picky eater, but thanks to Tres's upbringing around adventurous food, he introduced me to a world I never knew. I discovered not only did I love food I thought I would hate, but also that I had such an interest in it all. I wanted to learn more. The family cookbook my Mammaw passed to me and Tres persuading me to try new foods are the reasons I started cooking.

Our story started at work. I actually read that close to seventy percent of people meet their significant other at work. I don't know how accurate that statistic is, but for Tres and I, it was meant to be. Tres moved from Knoxville to Memphis after the company I worked for bought a company he helped start up. He told me he vowed to not get into a relationship because he wanted to focus completely on work but saw me walking down the hall in the office one day and thought, "Who is that?" A few weeks later, we ended up meeting at a co-worker's birthday party. I remember sitting down to talk to him and thinking we had only been chatting a few minutes, but when we looked up everyone was gone. Hours had passed and if our friends happened to bid either of us goodbye, we didn't even notice. A few days later, we had our first date. It wasn't long after, we learned we had a mutual love for travel, rock music and good ole fun with food and wine at the center of it all. As our relationship progressed, I remember thinking, "Wow, this is so easy." I remember Mama saying, "When he looks at you, there's love in his eyes." Over ten years later, I still see that look, and we genuinely have the most relaxed, exciting, love-filled life. We do everything together and it never gets old – travel the world, wine and dine, rock out to old music on our record player, paint the town red – even if it's just the two of us- it feels like a crowd of people. It can simply be us two, doing just about anything and we'll have a blast doing it.

If I had a big bottle of ice cream sprinkles, I could pick every morsel out and give a reason I love Tres. He's the reason life is so grand. I tell him all the time, "I love you so much, I burst inside." This chapter is full of desserts so delicious you'll burst inside – only fitting to dedicate it to your one and only, your happily ever after.

Rose Shortbread Cookies

Makes 20 to 25
cookies

Tres and I frequent Vegas. He travels there for work several times
a year and because I fell in love with it the first time he took me,
I invite myself along on a couple of his business trips. The first
time he took me, we had cocktails at The Chandelier Bar in the
Cosmopolitan Hotel. I ordered a cocktail that was described on the
menu as tasting "like a garden." When I took my first sip, I couldn't
believe what I was drinking – it was like walking through a rose
garden, only I was sipping it. That's when I fell in love with the
flavor of rose, a flavor I never even knew existed until that vacation.
These cookies are inspired by that cocktail – they're equally as
feminine and just as tasty.

Make the cookies. Preheat your oven to 350 degrees. Using a handheld or
stand mixer with a paddle attachment, beat together the butter, powdered
sugar, vanilla, and rose water extract on medium speed until completely combined
and fluffy. In a medium bowl, sift together the flour and salt. Slowly add the flour to
the sugar-butter mixture, mixing on low speed until the dough comes together.

Dump the dough onto a heavily floured surface, turn to coat in the flour, gather
into a ball, and then shape into a smooth, flat disk.
🕐 *Wrap in plastic wrap and chill in the refrigerator for at least 30 minutes or
up to one week.*
Using a rolling pin, roll the dough out to about ½-inch thick. Using heart-shaped or
circle cookie cutters, cut out the cookies and place on an ungreased baking sheet.
Bake for about 15 to 20 minutes, or until golden. Let cool.

Make the glaze. In a medium bowl, whisk together the powdered sugar, heavy
cream, and rose water extract. Dip the cookies into the glaze, face down, and place
on a clean baking sheet. Sprinkle the tops with sprinkles, if desired. Let the glaze
harden before serving.

COOKIES:

- 1 cup unsalted butter - room
  temperature
- ¾ cup powdered sugar
- ½ teaspoon vanilla extract
- ¾ teaspoon rose water
  extract
- 2 cups all-purpose flour, plus
  more for dusting
- ¼ teaspoon kosher salt

GLAZE:

- 1 cup powdered sugar
- 2 ½ tablespoons heavy
  cream
- ½ teaspoon rose water
  extract
- Pink or red sprinkles
  (optional)

Notes

Nenne's Famous Pecan Pie

Makes 2 crusts, 1 pie

My Nenne is so special to me. She loves life, is hilarious without even realizing it and always makes sure no matter where she is, she's having a ton of fun. Every holiday and special occasion, she makes her pecan pie because it's what everyone requests. One year, she was out of town for Thanksgiving, and everyone freaked out. Who in heaven's name would make the pecan pie? I had never made it but gave it a whirl. Since then, it's become my job to make the pie. Pecan pie is one of my favorite desserts, and I have never had one better than this.

Make the pie crust. In a large bowl, sift together the flour, salt, and sugar. Add the shortening and cold butter, then break it up with a pastry cutter, or quickly with your hands, until crumbly. Add ice water a little at a time until the flour mixture comes together. Continue to bring it together with your hands until smooth, being careful not to overwork it.

🕐 *Once a smooth ball is formed, cut the dough in half, wrap each half in plastic wrap, and refrigerate for at least 30 minutes or up to several days.*
Take out one of the dough balls, and on a heavily floured surface, pat the dough out into a disk shape. Continue flouring if the dough seems too sticky or fragile. Using a floured rolling pin, roll out the dough into a circle about 12 inches in diameter and press into a 9-inch pie pan. (The remaining crust can be frozen and used later.)

Make the pie. Preheat your oven to 350 degrees. In a small saucepan, bring the corn syrups and butter to a boil for 2 minutes. In a medium bowl, whisk together the sugar and eggs. Add the hot corn syrup mixture to the sugar mixture and stir together quickly. Add the nuts and vanilla and stir to completely combine. Pour the mixture into the prepared pie shell and bake for about 42 to 45 minutes. Before taking it out of the oven, shake the pie. If it's still very shaky, keep baking for an additional 5 to 10 minutes. The pie shouldn't come out of the oven until it's just slightly shaky and almost set. Let cool before serving.

CRUST:

- 2 cups all-purpose flour, plus more for dusting
- ¼ teaspoon kosher salt
- 3 tablespoon granulated sugar
- ¼ cup Crisco® shortening – cold
- 12 tablespoons unsalted butter – cold and cubed
- ¼ cup ice water, plus more if needed

PIE FILLING:

- ½ cup white and dark corn syrup (mostly dark, some white)
- ¼ cup unsalted butter
- 1 cup granulated sugar
- 3 large eggs – beaten
- 2 cups pecans
- 1 teaspoon vanilla extract

Notes

Vanilla Berry Shortcake

Serves 8

I insist on having a red, white and blue dessert for patriotic holidays such as Independence Day, Memorial Day, Veteran's Day and even when cheering on USA athletes in the Olympics. This red, white and blue dessert takes the cake – literally. It presents beautifully, and is a huge crowd-pleaser.

Make the shortcakes. Preheat your oven to 400 degrees. In a large bowl, whisk together the flour, baking powder, salt, and 3 tablespoons of the sugar. Using a pastry cutter or your hands, quickly cut the butter into the dry mixture until crumbly. In a liquid measuring cup, place 1 cup of the heavy cream, vanilla bean seeds, and vanilla extract. Mix together well so the vanilla bean seeds are broken up. Make a well in the center of the dry ingredients and pour in the heavy cream mixture. Fold everything together until the dough starts to form. Dump the dough onto a floured surface and knead the dough together until incorporated, being careful to not overmix. Press the dough out into a ¾-inch thick disk.

🕐 *Use immediately, refrigerate for several days or freeze for up to 2 months in plastic wrap.*

Using a large, round cookie or biscuit cutter, cut the dough into circles. Place on a baking sheet lined with parchment paper, brush the tops with the extra cream, sprinkle with sugar, and bake for about 12 minutes, or until golden. Let cool.

Assemble the dessert. In medium bowl, place the berries and the remaining 2 tablespoons sugar. Stir together and let the mixture sit at room temperature for at least 30 minutes to macerate. Using a handheld or stand mixer with a whisk attachment, make the whipped cream by beating together the heavy cream, powdered sugar, and dash of vanilla until firm. Cut the shortcakes in half, fill with the berries, and top with whipped cream.

- 2 cups all-purpose flour
- 1 tablespoon baking powder
- ½ teaspoon kosher salt
- 5 tablespoons granulated sugar, plus more for sprinkling
- 6 tablespoons unsalted butter - cold and cut into small cubes
- 2 cups heavy cream, plus more for brushing
- 1 vanilla bean - split, seeds scraped out
- ½ teaspoon vanilla extract, plus a dash
- 2 cups fresh berries – any kind you like or several different kinds
- 3 tablespoons powdered sugar

Notes

....
....
....
....
....
....

Delta Death by Chocolate Cake

Makes 1 double
layered cake

I was a cheerleader in college at Delta State University. At the time, the cheerleading program was one of the best in the country with several national championship titles and I received a scholarship to join the team. Practicing for nationals was time consuming. Often when the rest of the student body went home for holidays, we would stay and practice. I was too far from home to go back between practices, so one day I went home with a girlfriend on the team whose family had a farm in Clarksdale, Mississippi, only about a half-hour from the university. All I remember about that visit was the cake her mom made. She called it Death by Chocolate Cake. I'd never had anything so delightful! I loved it so much, I got the recipe from her and to this very day, this is the cake Mama makes me for my birthday. I re-created it ever so slightly to present on a cake stand.

- Unsalted butter, for greasing
- All-purpose flour, for dusting
- 1 box Devil's Food Cake mix, plus box ingredients
- 2 cups cold heavy cream
- ¼ cup powdered sugar
- ½ teaspoon vanilla extract
- ½ cup sweetened condensed milk
- 6 ounces Heath Bar candy crumbles

Notes

Preheat your oven to 350 degrees. Grease and flour the bottom and sides of 2 (9-inch) cake pans. Mix the cake together according to the box's directions. Pour evenly into the prepared baking pans and bake for 25 to 30 minutes, or until set. Let cool. Using a handheld or stand mixer with a whisk attachment, make the whipped cream by beating together the heavy cream, powdered sugar, and vanilla until soft peaks form.

When the cakes are cool, run a knife around the edges, then gently turn each one over onto a plate. Using a serrated knife, cut the tops off each cake, creating a flat surface. Transfer one of the cakes to a cake stand or platter. Spread the sweetened condensed milk in a thin layer evenly over the top. Then evenly spread half the whipped cream over that. Sprinkle with half the Heath Bar crumbles. Stack the other cake on top. Spread the remaining whipped cream atop and sprinkle the remaining Heath Bar crumbles over the top. Refrigerate until ready to serve.

Everything Candy Bar Milkshake

Serves 4 to 6

Tres jokes that his favorite day of the year is November 1st. It happens to be my brother's birthday, but the reason it's Tres's favorite is because it concludes my month-long, crazy Halloween celebrations. He's all like, "Hallelujah!"- and I'm crying. Just kidding, but really, I think it's the saddest day of the year. So I keep Halloween going with this sweet treat. Everyone has leftover Halloween candy, why not make a milkshake out of it? I throw various uneaten chocolate bars in, and it comes out 100 percent tasty every time. I bet your kids won't even get mad at you for stealing their candy to make this treat.

- 4 cups vanilla ice cream
- 1½ cups whole milk, plus more to thin the shake if desired
- 2 cups various leftover candy bars - roughly chopped

Place the ice cream, milk, and candy bar pieces in a blender. Close the lid and blend on high until smooth. For thinner milkshakes, add more milk. Serve in tall glasses with a straw.

Notes

Moon Pie Banana Pudding

Serves 8 to 12

Mama's banana pudding has been in the family as long as I can remember and to this very day, it's the best banana pudding I've ever eaten. I know, banana pudding is one of those desserts everyone claims their mama or grandmama has the best, but my Mama's really is the best! When I was a kid and would visit Nenne, she would often give my brother and me a couple of dollars to walk down the street to the general store and get any treat we wanted – one of my go-tos was a Moon Pie. Last Christmas, for laughs, Nenne wrapped up a box of banana-flavored Moon Pies for me to open and it was one of my favorite gifts! I decided I wanted to use them in a fun recipe creation, so I took Mama's banana pudding recipe and my beloved Moon Pie memories and threw them together to create the most delightful dessert. Aside from how scrumptious it is, my favorite part about this recipe is it can be whipped up in no time at all.

- 1 (3.5-ounce) box instant French Vanilla Pudding
- ½ cup whole milk
- 1 (14-ounce) can sweetened condensed milk
- 1 (8-ounce) container whipped cream
- 40 to 50 vanilla wafer cookies
- 3 bananas – sliced ½ inch thick
- 5 banana-flavored MoonPies

Notes

In a large bowl, whisk together the pudding and milk until smooth. Fold in the sweetened condensed milk and whipped cream until combined. Evenly line the vanilla wafer cookies on the bottom of an 8-inch baking dish and top with a layer of banana slices. Crumble two of the MoonPies over the bananas then smooth half the pudding mixture over the MoonPie crumbles. Make another layer of vanilla wafer cookies, banana slices, and crumbles from two more MoonPies. Top with the other half of pudding and decorate the top using the leftover vanilla wafer cookies and the remaining MoonPie.

Balsamic Blueberries with Lemon Cream

When hosting a dinner, I spend the most time on the main dish. I always assumed that was the most important part of a big dinner presentation – until I heard dessert is what everyone remembers from a dinner party. To be truthful, I often skipped dessert all together when it came to my parties, but now I know better. Because I spend so much time on the meal, I like to have a few simple, ready-to-go desserts in my back pocket. This one is ideal because it can be completely prepped before, in the fridge and ready to go when the last bite of dinner is taken.

Serves 4

- 3 cups blueberries
- 1 tablespoon granulated sugar
- 2 tablespoons white balsamic reduction
- Kosher salt
- ½ cup heavy whipping cream
- Zest of 1 lemon, plus more for garnish

In a medium bowl, place the blueberries, ½ tablespoon sugar, the white balsamic reduction, and a dash of salt.

🕐 *Stir to combine and set aside for at least 30 minutes or overnight to macerate.*

Using a handheld or stand mixer with a whisk attachment, make the whipped cream by beating together the heavy cream, lemon zest, and remaining ½ tablespoon of sugar until firm. Spoon the blueberry mixture into glass bowls or jars and top with whipped cream and a sprinkle of zest.

Notes

....

....

....

Whisky Peach Galette

When Tres and I lived downtown in Memphis, we walked to the farmer's market every Saturday morning from our condo on Main Street. It was Jones Orchard out of Millington, Tennessee, that made me fall in love with peach desserts. One of my favorite stops to this day is their stand where I load up on fresh peaches to make this delicious dessert. It takes no time to make and the whisky adds a little Southern zing, "adulting it up."

Preheat your oven to 400 degrees. In a medium sauté pan over medium-high heat, melt the butter. Add the peaches, lemon juice, and salt. Stir together and cook for one minute. Add the whisky and vanilla and cook for 2 to 3 more minutes, or until the whisky is reduced by half. In a small bowl, combine the sugar, cinnamon, and corn starch. Take the peach mixture off the heat and stir in the sugar mixture and the walnuts.

Lightly flour a clean work surface. Using a rolling pin, roll the puff pastry out into a large square until thin, being careful to not break the pastry. Using a large bowl (about 10 inches in diameter) as a mold, cut the puff pastry into a circle and place on a baking sheet. Pour the peach mixture in the middle of the circle and fold the edges over the top, overlapping each other – it doesn't have to be perfect, rustic is the key here. Brush with the beaten egg and sprinkle with sugar. Bake for 15 to 20 minutes. Let slightly cool and serve with vanilla ice cream or whipped cream.

Makes 1 large galette

- 1 tablespoon unsalted butter
- 2 peaches – pitted and sliced
- ½ lemon – juiced
- Dash kosher salt
- 3 tablespoons whisky or bourbon
- ½ teaspoon vanilla extract
- 3 tablespoons granulated sugar, plus more for sprinkling
- ½ teaspoon ground cinnamon
- ½ teaspoon corn starch
- ½ cup chopped walnuts
- 1 sheet puff pastry - thawed
- 1 large egg – beaten
- Vanilla ice cream or whipped cream – for serving

Notes

In winter months, the peaches can be replaced with pears.

LouLou's Bourbon Pound Cake

1 cake

This recipe comes from the grandmother of one of my best college girlfriends. Sara was the first friend I met at Delta State. We cheered together, were Phi Mu's together, and our friendship continued after college. A few years ago, she shared her grandmother Lou Lou's cookbook with me. It's a cherished family heirloom that was passed down to her. Much of the book is hand-written, and I found the recipes to be so unique and special – another reminder that Cooktales are alive and well. I told Sara I hope she has it locked in a fire-proof safe because this cookbook of hers is absolute antique gold! I am grateful for Sara's long-time friendship and these recipe treasures of family history she's shared with me over the years. This one is my favorite. It's great topped with any macerated fruit – whatever's in season when you make it.

- 1 pound unsalted butter or margarine
- 3 cups granulated sugar
- 8 large eggs – separated
- 3 cups all-purpose flour – sifted
- 1/3 cup bourbon
- 2 teaspoons vanilla extract
- 2 teaspoons almond extract
- ½ cup chopped pecans
- Powdered sugar, for sprinkling (optional)

Notes

Preheat your oven to 350 degrees. Using a handheld or stand mixer with a paddle attachment, cream the butter and 2 cups of sugar together until light and fluffy. Add the egg yolks, one at a time, beating well after each addition. Add the flour, alternating with the bourbon, vanilla extract, and almond extract, mixing until smooth. Stir in the nuts. In another bowl, gradually beat the egg whites until foamy. Add the remaining sugar to the whites and continue beating until stiff peaks form. Fold the egg whites into the batter. Pour into a well-greased 10-inch Bundt or tube pan. Bake for 1 hour and 20 minutes, or until cake pulls away from pan. Let cool. Turn over onto a platter or cake stand. Sprinkle with powdered sugar, if desired.

Watermelon Cream Sno Cones

There is the most fabulous, legendary little ice cream stop in Memphis called Jerry's Sno Cones. The line wraps around the place in the summer, and you want to cry on the days of the week it's closed. The sno cones there are the perfect mix of flavored shaved ice and the best ice cream you've ever eaten. Watermelon is and will forever be my favorite fruit in life and it's a solid flavor pick when making a stop at Jerry's. You always see berries, pineapple and other fruit as topping options and in ice cream recipes, but no one ever mentions watermelon. Why wouldn't the sweetest, juiciest fruit be a common ice cream topping? Because watermelon shaved ice IS a topping option at Jerry's, I decided to make my own version at home using fresh watermelon. I literally can't put into words how delicious this is! It's like having your own authentic Jerry's Sno Cone at home but with fresh watermelon!

Serves 4

- 4 cups cubed, seedless watermelon
- ¼ cup granulated sugar
- ¼ teaspoon kosher salt
- Squeeze of fresh lemon juice
- 4 cups vanilla ice cream

Notes

Freeze the watermelon cubes in a ceramic bowl or pan for at least one hour. Transfer the frozen cubes to a blender and blend together with the sugar, salt, and lemon juice until liquified. Pour the mixture back into the ceramic bowl or pan and freeze for 1 hour. Using a fork, break up the partially frozen mixture. Freeze 1 more hour, or until set. Remove from the freezer, and, using a fork again, break up the mixture until slushy, icy flakes form. Spoon 1 cup of ice cream into 4 separate bowls and top with the icy watermelon.

Reminisce & Relish
Your Keepsake Recipes

ACKNOWLEDGMENTS

Since the start of my cooking career, there has been so much support and so many people cheering me on - for that I am so grateful. This book would simply not be possible with me alone, and *Andrea's Cooktales* would not exist or mean anything without my family and friends.

FAMILY. Thank you so much to my mom, Mama, who has been my number one hero and inspiration from the beginning and gave us the most cherished childhood full of excitement, fun and stories - everyone on earth deserves a mom just like you, the world would be a better place. To Cliff, my Pop, for treating me like his favorite daughter from the very first day and always being there, without a question, for anything and everything. To my brother, RT, for childhood memories that will never be forgotten and new ones we continue to make as adults - and to Jennifer, the best sis-in-law, who is always willing to be along for the ride and puts up with our constant energy. To Nenne, I've always looked up to your zest for life and vibrancy - you're the life of the party and the most fun and funny grandmother a gal could have. To Jesse, thank you for putting up with Nenne and the rest of us nuts. To Gina, Kirk, Melissa, Riley and Brett for family memories new and old and bringing a little Texas to Mississippi and Tennessee. To Carol, for being such a happy, positive, good-natured mama-in-law who always does good and never has anything bad to say. To Frank and Judy for the ever-inspiring travel stories - Tres and I hope to live them all out some day - and for always having a food spread in your home that gets my wheels turning. To Renee and Alex for using your amazing talents to take a chance on Andrea's Cooktales - the video series, for making me look better than I am, always making me feel like anything is possible and for loving food as much as Tres and I do. A special thank you to the Tatum side of the family who inspired *Andrea's Cooktales* in so many ways. Thank you to Mammaw and Sheila for passing me the family cookbook - it gave me the best ravioli recipe in the world, taught me to cook, showed me there's so much history when it comes to food, and that the best family stories remembered are in the kitchen and at the dinner table.

FRIENDS. A big thank you to each one of y'all who have been my taste testers - I feel like I'm putting y'all through a lot sometimes, but something tells me you don't mind much. For all my dinner table lingerers - you all know I can sit, eat, drink, laugh and be merry for hours on end, thanks for understanding that obsession and eating slowly with me. To every friend who has traveled with me and put up with my endless obsession of finding the best places to eat "that may inspire my next story," thank you for letting me drag you down every weird alley, through every nook and cranny and around in circles until we find the most special spots - you know who you are, and I'm so grateful for you all. To Ginger and James for being a part of so much in our lives - y'all are our adventurous travel partners and the official taste testers. To "the girls" - Ginger, Sara, Tracy and Amy Claire - you have listened to me blather about my blog, business and cookbook, and given me advice on all of it for years - thanks for always lending your ears and having the most honest opinions. Bethany, you may not even realize it but you're the best publicist I'll ever have - I can't thank you enough for your constant cheerleading, for shouting *Andrea's Cooktales* from the rooftop, and for introducing me to everyone (because I'm pretty sure you know *everyone*). A special thank you to Facebook and Instagram friends and supporters - no comment, message, share or like goes unnoticed.

TEAM. I'm so grateful to work with people who are not only talented, smart and passionate, but also enjoyable, enthusiastic and so very supportive - believing through and through in *Andrea's Cooktales*. Thank you to Susan Schadt, a publisher so brilliant, for taking a chance on me and turning this book into more than I could have ever imagined my first book to be - you've brought it to life, thanks for pushing me to make the right decisions and putting up with my more often than not indecisiveness. Jennifer Chandler, I am just so glad we met - you have been such an amazing influence to have on this journey, and I can't thank you enough for all the advice, ideas, and for being as thrilled to read through *Andrea's Cooktales* as I was to write them. To Nicole Cole, the one and only photographer (and assistant food stylist) I knew without a doubt could bring this book to life - you surpassed it beyond my wildest dreams, and I'm thankful for not only your beautiful work but also constant prayers, reassurance, friendship and faith in it all from the very beginning. To Corrie Blair and Ryan Slone, graphic designers who turn pictures, recipes and stories into magic on a page - thank you for laying out a book that makes me want to jump up and down and cheer every time I flip through.

MY LOVE. To Tres, my sweet, this is all you - every single page. Honestly, none of it would be possible without your unconditional love and support, advice, ideas, taste buds and willingness to travel and try everything. Every single day is like living inside the best dream because of you. I love you so much my heart bursts. Also, thank you to our best boy, Rufus, for sitting on my lap and being the best cuddle buddy while I write and for staring at me, hoping food drops, while I cook.

INDEX

BIOS

ANDREA LETARD is the creator of Andrea's Cooktales, a recipe blog, video series and cooking brand offering services as a recipe developer, personal chef, small party caterer and cooking instructor. Her recipes are what she calls "next-generation southern" – fun and fundamentally southern with a modern twist using fine, fresh and unexpected ingredients. She has been featured on the Cooking Channel, the Today Show, Local Memphis Live, and was chosen as a Top 100 Contestant on *MasterChef* Season 6. She has a master's degree in journalism and uses her writing background as a culinary contributor and recipe writer for various magazines. Her work has been featured in *4Memphis*, *Click*, *Memphis Health and Fitness*, *Good Health*, *FIX* and *American Cheerleader*. She lives in Memphis, Tennessee, with her husband, Tres and their dog, Rufus Orleans.

Follow her on Facebook, Instagram (@andreas_cooktales), and watch her video blog series at andreascooktales.com.

NICOLE COLE is a photographer, specializing in couples, food and lifestyle. She enjoys being a storyteller through photography, giving life to the dreams and stories of others. She lives with her husband and children in North Mississippi.

SUSAN SCHADT, editor and publisher, founded Susan Schadt Press in 2015. Additional books she has edited and published include: *First Shooting Light: A Photographic Journal Reveals the Legacy and Lure of Hunting Clubs Along the Mississippi Flyway* (2008), *Wild Abundance: Ritual, Revelry and Recipes of the South's Finest Hunting Clubs* (2010), *A Million Wings: A Spirited Story of the Sporting Life Along the Mississippi Flyway* (2012), *MEMPHIS: Sweet, Spicy and a Little Greasy* (2014), *The Chubby Vegetarian: 100 Inspired Vegetable Recipes for the Modern Table by Justin Fox Burks & Amy Lawrence* (2016), *Reel Masters: Chefs Casting About with Timing and Grace* (2016), *Calling The Wild: The History of Arkansas Duck Calls, A Legacy of Craftsmanship and Rich Hunting Tradition* (2017) and *Shelby Farms Park: Elevating a City, The Improbable Journey of America's Great 21st Century Urban Park* (2017).

www.susanschadtpress.com

Published in 2018 by Susan Schadt Press
Memphis | New Orleans

© 2018 by Andrea LeTard

Photographs © 2018 Nicole Cole

Text and design © 2018 Susan Schadt Press
Designed by DOXA

Library of Congress Control Number: 2018937471

ISBN 978-0-9973559-7-0

Printed by Friesens, Altona, Canada